MW01699456

Grand Delusions: Henry Hoet and Cobblestone Manor

Grand Delusions: Henry Hoet and Cobblestone Manor

James Musson

Brightest Pebble
Publishing Co. Inc.
1995

To Alice

First Printing, June 1995 by:
Art Design Printing Inc., Edmonton Alberta, Canada

Cover design by James Musson

First published in 1995 by
Brightest Pebble Publishing Co. Ltd.
7604 - 149 Avenue
Edmonton, Alberta, Canada
T5C 2V7
Telephone and Fax (403) 457-7496

Canadian Cataloguing in Publication Data

Musson, James, 1933-

Grand Delusions: Henry Hoet and Cobblestone Manor

Includes bibliographical references and index

ISBN 0-9699669-0-3

1. Hoet, Henry. 2. Artisans—Alberta—Biography. 3. Cobblestone Manor (Cardston, Alta.) 4. Cardston, (Alta.)—Buildings, structures, etc. 5. Cardston, (Alta.)—Biography. 6. Cardston (Alta.)—History. I. Title

NK2443.H64M88 1995 971.23'402'092 C95-900492-0

This book is based mainly on the memories of people who wittnessed first hand the events told in this book or who knew people who did. I recognize the problem of accuracy in memory reaching back a half-century and more. Therefore, I cannot guarantee that everything written in this book is accurate. I took some liberties and made some assumptions based on information that was not always complete.

Contents

Acknowledgments

THIS book would not have been possible without the kind co-operation of numerous people. I am grateful to the following for assisting me with my research. They gave generously of their time, their priceless memories, their friendly interest, and their eagerness to help me in every way. They appear in alphabetical order: Shiela Abercrombie, Laura L. Barrus, Ethel Beck, Rojanea (Jacobs) Bingham, Willard Brooks, Lila Cahoon, Bringham Young Card, Bill Dawson, Randall W. Dixon, Archivist, Historical Department, Salt Lake City, Utah, Ray Djuff of the *Calgary Sun,* Joe Durocher, Ed and Arlene Flickinger, Dr. Alan Gordon, Ivy Gregson, Maxine Hansen of Bird's Eye Ranch, Lyman H. Jacobs, Dr. Sybesma Jetske of the University of Alberta Dept. of Art, Karl Leszynski, Dr. Violet Meyers, Alice Musson, Elaine Nelson, Grant Payne, Willis Picher, Pat Pettitt, Nan Pitts, Bill Raistrick, Gene Salway, Harold A. Salway, Marion Schmilke, Rose Sinclair, Randy Smith, Reginald H. Smith, Howard Snyder, Rebecca Still, Leo Stutz, Hope (Salway) Swendsen, Shem Williams, Eda Wood, Forest Wood, V. Wood, Mable Workman, and Rachel H. Young, Rod Yukes.

I am also grateful to the following institutions that afforded me valuable information, their time and courtesy: Alberta Education, Alberta Hospital Edmonton (Oliver), Alberta Hospital Ponoka, Andrews-McLaughlin Funeral Home, Cardston Library, the Church of Jesus Christ of Latter-day Saints Historical Department, Edmonton Public Libraries, Glenbow Museum and Archives, National Archives of Canada, Provincial Archives and Waterton Natural History Association.

The production of this book was funded in part by the ALBERTA HISTORICAL RESOURCES FOUNDATION

Preface

THIS is not the book I originally set out to write. It gradually emerged while researching material for a book about unique homes, built by their owners with local or recycled materials. I knew of many examples and, in April 1994, I set out from Edmonton to visit several of these homes. Cobblestone Manor was one of them.

I had visited Cobblestone Manor on other occasions. It has been a restaurant for many years. On my frequent travels through Cardston, Alberta, I usually made it a point to stop there to enjoy its incomparable beauty, friendly atmosphere, and fine cuisine. I also enjoyed hearing about the reclusive European who built it. But, what I was really interested in was the technical aspect of its construction.

Ed and Arlene Flickinger, the owners and operators of Cobblestone Manor, were delighted by the prospects of having the house included in my book. They graciously conducted me on a personal tour and provided me with as much information about the house and its builder as they had. But, the information was sketchy, because the builder was reclusive and seldom communicated with anyone.

He was a Belgian of Flemish descent. Local residents say that he began building the house for his sweetheart in Belgium who had promised to join him upon its completion. When the house was nearly finished, he went insane and was committed to a mental hospital in Ponoka, Alberta. It was widely believed that his condition was caused by his sweetheart's refusal to join him and that he died shortly after entering hospital.

It all sounded like myth and hearsay to me, and some of it was. Nevertheless, my curiosity was aroused, and it launched me on a voyage of discovery that uncovered mystery, awesome wonder, constant surprise, sublime beauty, and deep tragedy. But not one scrap of information came easily. The reclusive builder left behind no written material—no diary, no journal, no letters, no bills. No one knew anything about his background and, it seems that he took care not to leave any trails. The search for information was replete with cul-de-sacs, but now and then a small bit of information surfaced, providing a breakthrough that would reveal new horizons and mysteries.

My odyssey transported me into the memories of people in their seventies, eighties and nineties. Some were in rest homes, but most of them held vivid memories of the man with the European accent who built the Rock House when they were young. It transported me into the minds of retired Alberta Hospital Edmonton personnel who once cared for the builder, but never believed him when he told of his achievements—the building of his mansion and the finishing work he did in Cardston's Mormon Temple, and Waterton's Prince of Wales Hotel. To his care givers, his claims were merely manifestations of his delusions of grandeur.

He died a forgotten man more than twenty years after being committed to hospital. He now rests in an unmarked grave in Edmonton. Cobblestone Manor, the monument he left behind, is now a designated Provincial Historic Site and tourist attraction.

This book is an effort to resurrect the memory of a great Alberta artist who has not been accorded the credit he deserves. It is largely based on the memories of those who knew or knew of him more than a half century ago. But memory is never perfect, and, what we think we remember is often "refabrication" of what we later see and hear about the original event. In spite of that, the stories told by a large number of people interviewed were strikingly similar.

Nevertheless, I recognize the possibilities of inaccuracy in this book. To tell the story of an artist who was in danger of being lost to posterity, I took some liberties and made some assumptions based on information that was not always complete. I used what objective information I had, but primary sources were seldom available. I do not know what went through the builder's mind, but I do know the nature of his disease. I know of his obsessions and desires, and the work he left behind. From these, I have interpolated thoughts that probably dwelled in his mind. Where information was sketchy, I let the environment tell the story.

I hope this book will serve as a springboard from which others will produce a complete and accurate picture of this complex man.

1. Builders and Pioneers

A short distance off the main street near the edge of Cardston, Alberta, stands a rambling two-story cobblestone house. Through heavy foliage, five gables peer out in various directions. Two rock chimneys emerge from a cedar shake roof and point relentlessly to the prairie sky. The entire four hundred sixty-five-square-metre edifice nestles in graceful elegance behind lilac bushes and several varieties of trees. This venerable fourteen-room manor once overlooked Lee's Creek from which came the rocks enclosing its unique interior. It is known today as Cobblestone Manor. The creek flows a little further from the house than it did when it was first built. Its course and depth were changed to prevent the flood damage that often occurred in the past to homes built too close to the creek.

People once called Cobblestone Manor the "Rock House." Others referred to it as the "Wonder House." To some it was the "Ghost House." Whatever name people gave it, the house was and remains an object of charm, grace, beauty, and curiosity. It evokes wonder, awe and, in the past, fear, because people in the community believed that it was haunted by its sole builder—an enigmatic recluse who worked obsessively on it for fifteen years.

There is something about Cobblestone Manor that resembles a living organism. It usurped the character of its builder and became the emporium of his dreams and illusions, congealed in rock, wood, and glass. His breath permeates the structure even though he is long dead. The oil from his skilled hands penetrate every piece of material used in the building. Every square centimetre is alive with his spirit; its existence stands as a manifestation of his creative mind.

Today Cobblestone Manor is a Provincial Historic Site. It is also a fine restaurant owned and operated by Ed and Arlene Flickinger since 1977. Here, you can relax in unique dining rooms, intricately decorated with thousands of small pieces of exotic hardwoods, inlaid in honeycombed ceiling and wall panels. You can enjoy traditional and exotic cuisine in the atmosphere of a European manor house.

The builder never enjoyed such fine fare while living and working in Cardston. Every cent he earned went into his Rock House, while his meals consisted of bologna, peanut butter, jam, and the occasional homemade meal or fresh baked bread from a generous neighbour who feared for the health of this stoic artist.

No one in the community knew much about the builder, except that he came from Belgium and was an artist in the truest sense of the word—a genius, recognized by those who viewed and understood his work. His name was Henry Hoet, a loner who seldom spoke or mixed with the people living in the community. He had not always been reclusive, but, for reasons unknown, he had become reticent in his new country.

With a castaway bicycle seat, Pablo Piccasso created a masterpiece. Henry Hoet did no less. From rubble, scrap materials, an artist's eye, and fifteen years hard labour, he created a dream house. The lot upon which the house took form was his canvas; nature provided the rest. When it was nearly completed, he was taken away to a mental institution. He would never see his creation again, and the town folks would never see him again. In the former case, the artist won fame, fortune, and immortality. In the latter, Henry Hoet disappeared into anonymity, not to be discovered again until almost a half century after his death.

Henry Hoet was Flemish, born in Antwerp, Belgium, in about 1880. Nothing is known about his childhood or his family except that his father's name was Richard. In Cardston, Henry never talked about family. Ed Flickinger, one of the present owners of Cobblestone Manor, was once told that Henry may have been a remittance man, exiled for shaming his aristocratic family, but that can't be confirmed. It would, however, account for his extravagant taste in decor and his love of aesthetic interior surroundings.

Apparently, he apprenticed as a cabinetmaker before leaving Antwerp, aboard the Red Star Line's *S.S. Vaderland* on November 23, 1907. He arrived in New York City on December 3, of the same year. He was twenty-seven years old and single. Some of Cardston's old-timers say that he worked in a piano factory in New York City.

Henry knew New York City. He had first come to the Big Apple in 1905 and lived there until 1907, when he returned to Antwerp. But his stay in Europe was brief and he again obeyed the beck and call of the New World. He re-entered the United States as a non- immigrant alien, suggesting that he came to the

United States to work or visit, not to become a U.S. citizen. He paid his own passage and arrived with more than the minimum fifty dollars required to enter the country. He was young, literate, cultured, skilled, financially solvent, and full of adventure.

He moved in with a friend, Charles Ferriano, at 249 W. 27 Street, close to the city center and all of Manhattan Island's sights, sounds, flavours and action: Fifth Avenue, Broadway, Madison Avenue, Central Park, Times Square. He became immersed into the heart of New York—the emporium of dreams, the cornucopia of expectations, the melting pot of Babylon.

When Henry arrived, the United States was suffering from another of its cyclic depressions, and New York City was on the verge of bankruptcy. But it was also a time of great financial moguls who could, with a word, bring financial opulence or ruin to a country. New York needed help and J. Pierpont Morgan could and did re-finance the struggling city, which meant next to nothing to Henry Hoet. He moved in an environment of motorbuses and electric trolley cars within a din of popular music: "Dark Eyes," "Glow Worm," "On the Road to Mandalay," "Cuddle Up a Little Closer," "Shine on Harvest Moon," "Take Me Out to the Ball Game," "It's a Long Way to Tipperary," and other such titillating tunes. Cracker Jack, Coca Cola, Canada Dry Ginger Ale was being gobbled and swigged by millions while President Theodore Roosevelt puffed himself up like an adder, rattled his sword, and preached the gospel of "manifest destiny." In spite of the maniacal madness of Adam Smith's *laissez faire,* make-and-bust economic chaos, nearly 1.29 million immigrants streamed into the United States. Henry moved about the milieu but was not part of it.

Why and when he left New York City is not known, but he disappeared from the Big Apple only to reappear, like a ghost from nowhere, in Cardston, Alberta. It was about the farthest place he could get from Belgium without settling somewhere like the Kamchatka Peninsula in Eastern Siberia. Some say he arrived in 1911, but no one still living can verify that. No one really knows how he got there, or where he lived before buying the site upon which he built his house, or why he came to the predominantly Mormon settlement on the prairies, far from the big metropolitan cities he knew so well. He brought no mementos from the past and apparently wanted none; except one. He claimed to be engaged to a young lady he left behind in Belgium, while he came to the New World to make a new life. He planned for her to join him, when he got settled and could provide a home for her. Then they would marry.

Henry was in his early thirties when he arrived in Cardston. He knew no one in town and he was not Mormon. He was Catholic. Some, who were acquainted with him, say he came to work on the Mormon Temple. Construction began in 1913, but the finishing work, at which Henry was expert, didn't start until much later. He may have worked as a labourer or rough carpenter in the interim, but records show that his employment was sporadic. One has to wonder how he made his living before finally gaining steady employment as a finishing carpenter in the temple.

Cardston was a bustling, progressive community that seemed to have spontaneously generated itself overnight on an empty prairie far from the rest civilization. Its auspicious beginning came as a result of desperate people in search of a place where they could freely practice their religion.

Many of the founders of Cardston were alive and flourishing when Henry arrived. They were members of the Church of the Latter-day Saints, better known as the Mormon Church. Joseph Smith founded the faith on April 6, 1830, at Fayette, New York. Through a series of misadventures and religious persecutions, a vanguard of Mormon settlers, led by Brigham Young, settled in Utah in 1847 at a place now known as Salt Lake City. Other members followed, coming from many parts of the United States and Europe. They created settlements throughout Utah under Young's leadership.

Their settlements expanded like a geometric progression as more and more converts converged on the wastelands of Utah. They came by every mode of transportation, including the famous handcart expedition in which masses of immigrants and converts, pushed handcarts, loaded with their worldly possessions, across the vast prairies to the promised land. Others came in wagons or on horseback. They took up land and seeded crops where nothing domestic had ever before taken root. With the magic of hard work, irrigation, and faith, crops grew and the land was transformed into a rich and productive Zion.

In 1849, the settlers applied for statehood under the name of Deseret, meaning "honeybee." The term signified the industry of the people. The U.S. government rejected the application. Between 1856 and 1887, the Mormons made five more efforts to gain statehood. Washington rejected them all.

By the time the 1870s rolled around, most of the productive land was taken, but the faith continued to expand with more and more converts. They were becoming victims of their own constant success.

Mormonism was not all that was expanding. So was the United States, especially with the impetus of the California gold rush and, later, the completion of America's first transcontinental railroad in 1869. The general acceptance of the belief in manifest destiny also had something to do with U. S. expansion. With the western movement of American settlers came the same intolerance that had originally driven the Mormons out of their earlier settlements in the eastern and midwestern United States and cost them their leader, Joseph Smith. He was murdered by a mob on June 27, 1844, while he occupied a jail cell in Carthage, Illinois. People were suspicious of the Mormon's unorthodox co-operative society, ruled by an ecclesiastical oligarchy. The more their population grew in any one of their settlements, the greater the threat perceived by their neighbours.

To further provoke existing animosity, the Mormon faith appeared to appeal more to women than to men. That resulted in a population skewed toward more female members. Since the family was fundamental to Mormon life, there seemed to be a natural inclination toward polygyny (the practice of having more than one wife at any one time) to guarantee the opportunity of wedlock to all of its members. The King James Bible itself is filled with examples of great figures maintaining more than one wife, and the practice wasn't condemned. So, what was the problem? Well, other Christian religions for starters. They couldn't get away with that, so why should the Mormons?

The practice of polygyny seemed to give pious Americans sufficient cause to harass and persecute peaceful and productive people, even though polygyny was never common among most Mormons. It was just too expensive for the ordinary guy. Most Mormons maintained a monogamous relationship, and, after 1890, the Mormon Church no longer sanctioned polygyny. They ended the practice because of the heavy pressure the U.S. government brought to bear on them.

The U.S. Congress had enacted two pieces of legislation inimical to the continuation of polygamy (the practice of having more than one spouse at any one time). Both Acts were directed against the Mormon establishment. The first was the passage of the Edmunds Act in 1882, making polygamy punishable by heavy fines and imprisonment. This Act drove many Mormon Church members into hiding. Others sought places of refuge outside the U.S.

In 1887, the U.S. Congress passed the Edmunds Tucker Act, placing further restrictions on those practicing polygamy. Under this Act, the Mormon Church lost its corporate status, putting all church property in danger of being confiscated by the government.

The government was preparing the way for Utah statehood, but the Mormons posed a problem. Three conditions had to be met before the U.S. would grant Utah statehood: the Mormon Church would have to get out of politics, withdraw from an economic policy in which Mormons dealt primarily with each other, and discontinue the practice of polygamy.

Scarcity of farmland and government harassment prompted Mormon Church leaders to look abroad for undeveloped areas, where their people could establish new settlements, free from harassment.

Charles Ora Card, a son-in-law of Brigham Young, was a prominent church leader and resident of Logan, Utah. He was also a fugitive being sought by U.S. marshals for practicing polygyny. He had four wives. His first wife did not particularly relish a twenty-five per cent claim on her husband (less than that when religious and business interests are included) and filed for divorce. After their separation, she would notify the U.S. marshal every time she learned of her ex-husband's whereabouts.

Card considered fleeing to Mexico where he might establish a new settlement, but John Taylor, president of the Mormon Church, persuaded him to go to Canada instead. Joseph Smith Jr. had himself served as a missionary in Upper Canada. So had Brigham Young. Taylor had also served there and felt that Canada would receive Mormon settlers with justice and fair treatment.

Card accepted Taylor's advice, and, on September 14, 1886, he and two traveling companions, James W. Hendricks and Isaac E. D. Zundell, left Logan, for Canada.

The search for a suitable settlement, where farmland could be irrigated, started in British Columbia's Okanagan Valley. There, Card and his companions came across a mountaineer named MacDonald. He advised Card to take a look at southern Alberta's "buffalo plains covered with grass and miles of fertile soil."

Accepting the advice, Card and his friends rode off to Alberta, where they explored a number of possible areas for settlement. They found a suitable site located between the Belly and Waterton rivers in the Stand Off vicinity, next to the recently established Blood Indian Reserve. Being located only about forty kilometres southwest of Lethbridge was an added bonus.

Greatly satisfied, the party returned to Utah and reported to President Taylor. He confirmed their selection, after which Card immediately began recruiting volunteers for a new settlement in Canada.

At first, enthusiasm was contagious. Forty families agreed to pull up stakes and join the adventure, but on further reflection the numbers diminished to ten families. The romance of starting a new life in a new land was captivating, but to leave everything for which they had worked so hard over the years, including friends and family, was daunting. So, when D-day came, only ten hearty families answered the call.

Card led an advance party to the site on which they planned to establish their new settlement. When they arrived, they were shocked to learn that the land they had counted on had been leased to the Cochrane Ranch Company and was no longer available to them. There was nothing to do but to look elsewhere. Fortunately, friendly Albertans living in the area told Card about land that might be available near Lee's Creek, about seventy-five kilometres southwest of Lethbridge. Card and six other men scouted the area and found it a suitable alternative. On April 26, 1887, he laid claim to the land that would be their new settlement. It occupied an area about five kilometres upstream from where Lee's Creek enters the St. Mary's River, twenty-five kilometres from the U.S. border and south of the recently established Blood Reserve. On June 3, 1887, nine wagons arrived and forty-one settlers began building a new community. It would later be named Cardston.

Through the summer and fall, the settlers laboured diligently. By the time winter rolled around, ten log cabins had been built. By January, a twenty-foot-square log structure was completed. It served as the first meeting house, school, chapel, and a place for community entertainment. A church-based co-operative started in 1888 and included a store, sawmill, cheese factory, and flour mill.

Church officials in Salt Lake City helped the new settlement in every possible way, especially financially. They put up the money to buy the site on which Cardston was built. Then in 1889, they bought 9,840 acres of land near Cardston. At first, the land was used for a church ranch. Later it was divided into parcels and sold to settlers.

C. Edgar Snow established the first bank in 1895, and the *Cardston Record* (later the *Cardston News*) began publishing the same year. About two years later, the settlers developed the region's first successful irrigation system on the St. Mary's River. A sugar beet industry followed.

In December 1898, "Card's Town" was officially recognized as a village. Less than three years passed when Cardston, in what was then the North West Territories, became incorporated as a town. Charles Ora Card became its first mayor.

At first, Cardston served as a refuge to Mormons seeking a place to escape persecution. That was the primary rational for its establishment. Economic possibilities lured later arrivals, because, under Mormon auspices, Cardston grew and flourished.

Settlers continued to stream into the area. By 1901, the towns of Magrath, Sterling, and Raymond had emerged. The villages of Leavitt, Taylorville, Woolford, Pershing, Jefferson, Del Bonita, Rinard, and Twin River were settled. From the original forty-one settlers, the population of Mormons in the area swelled to three thousand. Eleven hundred lived in Cardston.

Also in 1901, Edward J. Wood arrived in Cardston from Salt Lake City where he was born and raised. He arrived with his wife Mary Ann and his three children. In 1903, he was selected president of the Alberta Stake, a Mormon territorial jurisdiction comprising a group of wards. From then on, his destiny was to become one of the tireless driving forces to promote the Mormon community in Alberta. He devoted his long life to that end.

In May of the following year a devastating flood substantially altered the face of Cardston. Lee's Creek overflowed, leaving many people homeless. A bridge on Main Street washed away. Gravel and trees, broken timbers, and rubbish covered the once picturesque tree-lined streets. On July 1, a second and worse flood raged through the town, this time ruining every building site along Lee's Creek. At one site, this auspicious event supplied the rubble material that would one day become one of Cardston's most important tourist attractions—Cobblestone Manor.

Cardston became more accessible when the A.R.&I. Railroad came to town in 1904. It was the first standard gauge train that ever ran into Cardston. It set off a building boom. The fifty-room Cahoon Hotel, built in 1905, was the most conspicuous development in the town. It became one of the first landmarks and the only first-class hotel in Cardston for years. It provided space for the Royal Bank of Canada and several offices. Locally quarried stone adorned the lower level in which a grocery store and hardware store opened. The hotel also became home to the Black and White Barber Shop, the Ideal Beauty Shop, a dental office, and a CPR telegraph office.

In 1906, Alberta Stake President Edward J. Wood, on behalf of the Mormon Church, bought the 66,500-acre Cochrane Ranch for $6.50 an acre. Much of this land was sold to settlers. From it sprung the communities of Glenwood, Hillspring, and Hartly.

Excavation began on the Spencer Hotel in 1911. It would house offices, seventeen hotel rooms, and a large auditorium. Other businesses appeared as if overnight: a newspaper, a meat market, a pharmacy, general store, and many more. Cardston had become a modern and thriving community.

By 1913, about seven thousand Mormons lived in the area and occupied most of the land. The stream of Mormon settlers to southern Alberta stopped. Into this Mormon milieu, Henry Hoet appeared and accomplished his greatest known work.

2. Icons In Rock

HENRY Hoet examined the two story log house with an expert eye. He found what he was looking for. The house was one of Cardston's oldest, having been built in 1889 by one of the first Mormon settlers, but it was solid and would make an excellent base for what Henry had in mind. It consisted of a kitchen about five metres square, a large living room of approximately the same size with a fire place, and two small bedrooms on the second floor.

The location, overlooking Lee's Creek, was perfect, but, it took an artist's eye to see the real potential. Devastation surrounded the stark dwelling owing to the terrible floods that had swept through Cardston years before, washing away the top soil and exposing more than an acre of cobblestones and sand. The house itself had not been damaged, as had so many others near by.

Most prospective buyers would have been repulsed by the ugly scene. Indeed, Joseph Young, the original owner, kept the house for only one year after the flood and then sold the blemished property to John T. Bateman, who had come with his family to Cardston from Utah in about 1899.

Henry, on the other hand, saw a unique opportunity. He had plenty of rocks and sand free for the taking. Instead of fretting about how to get rid of the debris, he conceived of how he could use it creatively to build one of the most wondrous houses in southern Alberta.

Joseph Young, sent to Cardston with his family by church officials to "assist in the establishing of a Mormon community," bought a property from John Anthony Woolf soon after his arrival in 1893, and began building the 22-by-44 foot log house, upon which Henry now gazed. It was one of the finest looking houses in Cardston at the time it was built.

It was also well built. By design or accident, Young had built the house of ten inch logs that had been fire-killed in a blaze that raged through a timber stand near Cardston in 1885. The fire naturally kiln-dried the timber that was left standing.

Nature had provided almost everything: a kiln-dried log house, rocks for walls, and sand and gravel for concrete and mortar. These materials were either on site or easy to reach. Moreover, someone, probably Bateman, had already weather-boarded the outside of the log walls.

Only time and effort were needed to turn the old log house into the Rock House. Its central core was in exceptionally good repair, being completely protected from the elements.

For two hundred dollars, Henry bought the house on the south side of Lee's Creek from Alice Viola Young of Preston, Idaho. Immediately upon taking possession he started its magic transformation.

Henry became an object of great curiosity in the community. Those still alive, who remember him, were children when he lived among them. Yet, like a photograph, his image remains burned in their minds. They describe him as being short—five feet, five inches tall—and stocky. His rumpled hair was dark, slightly curly and was thinning at the crown of his round head. He wore a thick black mustache. He was a serious man with a ruddy complexion and dark, intense eyes, and he spoke with a foreign accent. He seldom talked to anyone, and when he did, he spoke in such a quiet voice that it was hard to hear what he was saying. He was always polite, but withdrawn, and he never took part in community events. His constant companion was a large black Labrador dog. He never talked about himself or his family. About all anyone in Cardston came to know about him was that he was from Belgium and presumably had a sweetheart there (some thought a wife) who would join him when he could provide her with a home. What was her name? He never said.

During the time Henry lived in Cardston, he remained a mystery. He isolated himself behind a wall every bit as impenetrable as the cobblestones around which he sequestered himself. But there was one thing he could not hide—his genius.

In the same year Henry bought his house, construction began on an architectural masterpiece, the first Mormon Temple to be built in Canada. Henry Hoet played an important part in its construction.

Providence took a special interest in Cardston and intervened on its behalf. A desolate wasteland a mere quarter of a century before, Cardston became the object on which the Mormon Church, based in Salt Lake City, would bestow favours far in excess of those dealt other Mormon communities of similar size. Those favors reached a climax on February 9, 1913, when President Edward J. Wood received a letter from Brother Whitney, informing him that a temple would be built in Cardston.

The announcement brought much joy to Alberta Mormons but not surprise. Mormons believe in prophesy and, as early as June 19, 1887, the settlement's first Sunday school superintendent prophesied that a temple would be built in Canada. Later prophecies became more specific and placed the temple in the exact location it now occupies.

The stage was set. An obscure Belgian with strange habits, an inclination toward obsession, and a divine ability to create wonders with exotic hardwood just happened to be in the neighbourhood.

On November 5, 1913, construction began on the first Mormon Temple outside the United States with a ground-breaking ceremony. At around 2:00 in the afternoon, the faithful gathered at a desolate knoll, rising slightly above the rest of the sprawling town. The eight-acre block looked out on the purple silhouetted Rocky Mountains in the distance, standing like phantom sentinels to protect the yet unborn temple.

They conducted their simple ceremony in the autumn cold and sang, "How Firm a Foundation." Then they prayed. The president of the church, Joseph F. Smith, dedicated the eight-acre square, (Tabernacle Square) as the site of the new temple. Church dignitaries delivered speeches, followed by more prayers and the choir singing, "Our God We Raise to Thee." After the closing prayer, the first furrow was plowed.

Simultaneous with the building of the temple, Henry began building his own temple, dedicated to his own icon, his object of adoration half way around the world, his hoped-to-be wife. Each stone, laid with delicate care, would pave her way to him. It would be a magic temple—one she could not resist. Out of the ugly and commonplace, he would create a magnificent estate, using nothing but the finest materials. The accomplished product would make him worthy of her, or, at least acceptable.

But, was she real or merely a fantasy? Was she an imaginary link to a past he no longer acknowledged? Was her image a remedy for his loneliness in a foreign land with a strange people? Was she Dante's Beatrice leading him out of the commonplace into a dazzling brilliance? Why didn't this object of unrequited love have a name?

He worked on the temple and on his house with equal vigor and equal obsession. Nothing else mattered. He worked tirelessly, like a man possessed, forsaking all pleasures.

The weather was perfect during the fall and winter of 1913. New Year's Day of 1914 came and still no winter. Mormon volunteers continued to haul gravel for the temple as if it were September. Then a brief cold snap hit on January 18. The mercury dipped to -22°C, but the cold weather didn't last. Neither storms nor frost hindered the work. The project, that would consume ten years and create a monument of dazzling beauty, was underway.

The building of the temple had been estimated to take about one year, but war in Europe reduced the labour force and slowed construction. The cornerstone was not put into place until September 19, 1915. Standing in the mud under freezing rain and sleet, two thousand people witnessed the start of the million dollar temple that would earn Cardston the title as the "Temple City of Canada."

In the days that followed, the temple started to take the shape of a Maltese cross as designed by architects Hyrum Pope, a thirty-two-year-old German immigrant, and his twenty-five-year-old junior partner, Harold Burton of the firm Pope and Burton. Frank Lloyd Wright strongly influenced both men. Some of the meeting houses Pope and Burton had designed strongly resembled Wright's houses.

The temple would not only be one of its kind in Canada, it would be completely different from all other Mormon temples built up to that time. The traditional towers were eliminated, because they served no useful purpose. Instead the clean lines of a pyramid-shaped silhouette took form.

Originally, stone from a quarry near Cardston was considered for the temple. Several buildings in Cardston had been constructed of the local stone, but, upon further examination, church officials decided to look elsewhere. They finally agreed on granite from a quarry near Nelson, British Columbia. It was whiter and of finer grain than the local material.

The Kooteney Granite Company was contracted to supply the stone at fifty-five cents a cubic foot. Three thousand six hundred ninety tons of roughly cut white granite blocks were loaded on three hundred flatcars and delivered to Cardston. There, fine cutting and finishing was done, either at the railway station or at the temple site. Cranes unloaded the granite from the flatcars onto improvised wagons and horse drawn sleds called go-devils.

Teams and wagons hauled fourteen thousand cubic yards of sieved gravel with what the workers called dumpboards. The gravel was shoveled by hand. At times there were as many as thirty-two teams plying the dirt roads between the gravel pits and the building site. They also hauled fifty thousand bags of cement, and two hundred tons of steel. Spring was the most difficult season to transport supplies. Roads were soft and the wagons frequently bogged down to their axles. Sometimes granite chips were spread on the roads to firm them up.

One hundred railway cars from Canada Cement Company at Ekshaw, Alberta, each carrying a thousand bags of cement to be used in the temple building and its walkways, steamed into Cardston. Steel work was under contract to the Manitoba Steel Company of Winnipeg.

The building site and the area around it resembled an ant hill. Every form of conveyance was recruited and put into service. Many of the men, working on the temple, donated their time and teams of horses to haul gravel. Others donated to the project the proceeds from the sale of their hay and livestock.

According to church records, Henry probably didn't work continuously with the construction crew at the temple before 1918 or 1919. His forte was in the realm of special skills involving delicate finishing and inlay work. Before 1918, construction consisted primarily of excavation, concrete form making, concrete finishing, fireproof tile laying, and masonry work (cutting and fitting granite). The names of carpenters, masons, and labourers appear regularly in church ledgers, vouchers, and reports, but Henry's name occurs only occasionally.

Where his name does appear the record shows that he was among the highest paid employees on the job. Labourers were paid ten cents an hour, foremen thirty-five cents an hour and woodworkers forty-eight cents an hour.

Later records were not kept as precisely as earlier ones. They mention only the total monthly amount of the payroll without listing each individual on the labour force.

Four years after construction began, on September 23, 1917, a crew placed the capstone on the temple completing the outside construction.

Occasional work on the temple suited Henry. It gave him time to do the heavy outside construction on his house. As the outside structure of the temple progressed and took form, so did Henry's house.

His first project was to build a kitchen on the northwest side of the log structure, closest to the creek, where a coal shed with a dirt floor is believed to have been. He then turned his attention to remodeling the living room which he lined with hardwood paneling. Around the existing fireplace, he built book cases with stained-glass doors. Each door emerged as a work of art with fine woods and glass. He also created fixtures of wood and glass. He made floor and ceiling Tiffany lamps by cutting hexagonal and other shapes of stained glass imported from Italy and fitting them together with small strips of hardwood instead of lead. The same theme was carried from the bookcases and lamps into other fixtures. This room eventually became the library and is now the Henry Hoet room. Using fine oak, he built dining room chairs and perfectly balanced rockers, many of which can still be seen today at the Masons meeting hall and in many homes in Cardston and the surrounding area.

When the interior of the living room was finished, Henry began the task that gave the house its first name, the Rock House. He poured a concrete foundation around the house to support the stone walls, that he planned to erect around its perimeter.

Henry's dog served not only as a faithful companion, but as a valuable fellow worker. Harnessed to a cart fashioned by Henry, the dog hauled rocks from the creek to the building site. During the winter, a sled replaced the cart. When a sufficient supply of stones were gathered around the site, Henry washed each stone so they would bind properly. He then began laying the stone. Mixing the cement by hand, he applied the stiff concrete as a mortar and laid the stone wall against the existing structure.

Henry hired a local resident named Joseph Stutz with his team and wagon to help haul rocks. Joseph had gone into the drayage business after his farming venture in the area had ended in failure. He worked hard and long hours hauling gravel to various building sites at seventy-five cents a cubic yard. But he always seemed to find time to lend Henry a hand, hauling stones for his wonder house.

Joseph's young son, Leo, liked to go with his Dad. It made him feel grown-up and important to be working like a man along side Henry and his dad. But these adventures soon ended for the boy. Joseph had a certain feeling of apprehension about Henry and his eccentricities. Henry's speech was hard to understand. That could have been why he spoke so little and remained alone and reclusive. He always seemed to live in another world. He was obsessed with his work and often he appeared confused and dazed.

Joseph continued to help Henry when he could, but he felt uneasy about Leo being around him. There were times when Henry didn't seem quite right in the head, though Joseph would have been hard-pressed to cite any specific examples of unbalanced behavior. Nevertheless, he felt he couldn't be too careful. Recently, a man, believed to be mentally deranged, murdered a child in the neighbourhood. Joseph didn't want to take any chances and forbade Leo to go near Henry.

Henry was indeed an enigma in this closed Mormon community where everyone knew each other intimately; where every action was noted and every notable event recorded. It was not enough to know your neighbour and everyone else in the community, it was also important to know one's ancestors. Mormons take a particular interest in genealogy and have done more than any other group in the world to amass enormous amounts of genealogical data. In this environment, Henry was an object of curiosity, but the community treated him with respect and kindness. Some showed more than a little concern for his health, because Henry had the habit of neglecting himself. Sometimes he would forget to eat; often he would forget to sleep.

Gathering, hauling, washing, positioning, and securing each rock in place against the existing walls was a difficult task that took strength, skill, and patience. He was not a stone mason, and the rock layers that gradually covered the walls, did not display the sophistication of a professional mason, but that didn't matter. Its very roughness gave the building an earthy quality.

To keep the walls plumb, Henry used wood slabs as a form. This is the slip-form method. He laid the rocks in a line using the slabs as a brace. He would then mix his mortar and fill around the rocks, probably with his hands. The rocks were laid against the existing wall like a veneer.

Joseph Stutz probably helped Henry dig and pour a basement under part of the old house and the new room. Everything in the construction of Cobblestone Manor was unique. The basement was not an exception. Like most basements built at the time, Henry's was dark, dank, and ugly, but, unlike other basements, it was poured in layers with ten centimetre thick concrete shelves protruding about thirty centimetres from the wall. There are three of these seamless shelves surrounding the basement.

Another unique aspect of Henry's basement came to light. While Joseph was digging, he struck water. Actually, it was a spring. Henry hadn't planned on that, and, while a spring, gushing sweet water, can be a nice asset, it isn't when its in one's basement. Henry had no need of a spring springing eternal in his basement. Luckily, he had met a fellow by the name of Lee Gilchrist while working on the Mormon Temple. Gilchrist was employed as the hoist engineer, responsible for laying the stones for the walls of the temple. He had previously worked as a mechanic in a Cardston garage, and he had a special gift when it came to anything mechanical. He also had the answer to Henry's problem. Henry ended up buying a McLaughlin Buick engine from Lee to pump out his cellar.

Having completed the work on the original log house, the kitchen addition and the basement, Henry began another addition—a ten-by-twenty-two foot verandah on the south and east sides of the building. The walls of this verandah were of concrete with a cobblestone interior and exterior, and large windows made of small panes of glass.

He continued adding on rooms one at a time, but apparently, without any overall plan. Charley Beck, a man Henry worked with in construction, claimed that the general idea came from a house in Belgium that Henry had either worked on or lived in. The rooms took form around the original building, which served as the core.

The next room Henry added faced west and south. It would become the fifteen by thirty-seven foot dark oak room.

That was followed by a south-facing room. The sixteen by thirty foot room would later be paneled with golden oak. A large floor to ceiling bay window was included on the south wall opposite the fireplace. The materials for this room quite likely came from Lethbridge.

Finally, on the east side, an open verandah was added to tie the section together. This completed the outside walls of Henry's house. Before finishing the insides of the additions, he laid a rock wall against the entire structure.

Henry did not copy any particular style or school of architecture as he worked on his house, and he didn't put a name to the design. Once named, design becomes a style and takes precedence over thought. That could never be Henry's way. The direction the house took grew out of its original structure. It's progress was a reflection of the artist's mind in motion. Henry was the agent of its growth and change. He was designer, artistic director, and improviser.

3. The Alberta Temple

HENRY had been dividing his time between working on the temple and his house, but, after 1919 and the conclusion of the First World War, construction on the temple went into high gear. Not much had been accomplished on the temple during the war, but, at last, soldiers were returning home, and they found jobs working on the temple. Henry's skills were now needed full-time, and, he let the temple take precedence over his house because he needed money to buy materials, he loved working in the temple, and he was particularly favoured by his employer. Though he spoke little and then only in broken English, Henry's meticulous workmanship gave him a special status on the job, and with it the privilege of taking home scraps of exotic woods from all over the world. These materials added to the grandeur of his dream home. Henry gladly accepted them, knowing that if he didn't, they would be burned as trash.

Pope and Burton were the primary creators of the temple's interiors. The artists and artisans, selected to execute their designs, read like a *Who's Who* in Mormon avant-guard art. All were Mormons except Henry Hoet. He worked beside them all and took a back seat to no one.

Among the artists was A. B. Wright. He arrived in Cardston in 1919 to paint the murals in the chapel and baptistery. He had studied in Paris at the Julian Academie and the École des Beaux Arts. A professor of art at the Latter-day Saints University in Salt Lake City, he was noted for his landscapes and portraits and was considered one of Utah's most important art teachers. He also painted murals in the Hawaii and Arizona temples.

Torlief Knaphus was a sculptor from Norway. He began painting and carving at an early age. He attended the Royal Art School in Oslo, Norway, where he concentrated most of his efforts on sculpture. Later, he studied a year at the Paris Julian Academie under some of the world's most noted sculptors. He was about twenty-one years old when he joined the Mormon Church and immigrated to Utah. Besides the Cardston Temple, Knaphus found a home for his talent in the Arizona, Hawaii, Idaho Falls, and Los Angeles temples. He sculpted the oxen in the Alberta temple and later made models of that work to use in the baptismal font in the temple in Oakland, California.

Knaphus completed many other outstanding works of art emphasizing Mormon subject matter. They include the Hill Cumorah Monument, the Handcart Monument, and the School Children's Monument.

LeConte Stewart's paintings adorned the temple walls. He was known for his landscape paintings that numbered more than four thousand. He grew up in southern Utah and soon earned the title of the "Master of Mormon Landscape" and "Dean of Mormon Art." Besides his Mormon faith, he found God in nature. "With my canvas and brush," he said "I have learned to see beauty in every leaf and tree and hill. I have learned to love and respect His marvelous creations and have tried to keep in tune with Him."

Lee Green Richards painted the murals in the temple's Garden Room, using impressionist techniques. His treatment of foliage and peacocks played to the elements prevalent in the art nouveau movement, popular at the turn of the century. He depicted various kinds of wildlife living harmoniously in Eden-like serenity. His art also appears in the Idaho Falls Temple.

Edwin Evans, another well-known artist, was drawn to the Alberta Temple in the early 1920s. When he arrived, he was already in his sixties.

Joseph C. Shaw was responsible for the intricate plastering in the temple. He had joined the Mormon Church in 1910. According to his daughter, Laurene Shaw Sabey, Joseph would often "dream of the patterns at night and in the morning [he] was able to execute the moldings." Throughout his career, he worked for a number of contractors on many churches and public buildings in western Canada, always striving for perfection, always giving more than required. The highest point of his career was working on the Alberta temple.

These represent only a small number of the gifted people with whom Henry worked on the temple. Probably Henry's best contribution appeared in the Celestial Room. Trimmed to the ceiling with African Mahogany, the room exhibits exquisite inlay work.

In 1923, after many delays owing to war, cost overruns, bad weather, and other problems, the temple, planned to be finished by 1915 at the latest, was finally completed. Heber J. Grant, president of the Mormon Church in Salt lake City, came to

Cardston and dedicated the Alberta temple on August 26. It was the first Mormon temple to be built and dedicated outside the United States.

Its grandeur is awesome in its clean simplicity. Viewed from any angle, the temple rises majestically from its mound in stark, straight lines. Brilliant white walls of granite incline from four main and four lesser sides to the topmost point. The structure is octagonal—in the shape of a Maltese Cross. It is 118 feet square, supported on it's four sides by a ten-foot-high solid granite retaining wall, 165 feet square. It rises to a height of 85 feet.

The interior is known for its beautiful marble, and for hardwood from around the world: oak, ebony, maple, tulip, rose, African mahogany, and several kinds of walnut. All were expertly worked by skilled hands such as Henry's.

J. Y. Card described the temple in an article written for the *Lethbridge Herald*. He says: "Impressive and unique, it occupies a distinctive place of its own in the historic field of architecture. It has the Grecian massiveness, a Peruvian touch, and is similar only to the ancient temples of the Aztecs and other aborigines of South America... Of the nine temples erected by the Latter-day Saints, there is no other of similar exterior design."

4. Monument To Her

"Where your treasure is, there will your heart be also."
Luke 12:34.

AND so it was with Henry Hoet. But his house wasn't his treasure. It was merely a tool to obtain the treasure he really coveted—the unnamed lady he left behind in Belgium. That was the treasure he sought and, like a medieval knight, no sacrifice would be too great to do homage to his fair lady whether she be real or a figment of his quixotic imagination. The house would pour forth elegance and beauty consistent with the quality and excellence of his lady. Henry undertook a creative odyssey fully expecting that, at the end of the day, his Penelope would be the prize of his heroic effort.

He had a vision, and in his vision that nameless "her" stood with him within the profusion of beauty that he himself would create. That vision now became an obsession, and everything he did, he did for her.

Unlike most of the dwellings that were built primarily for utilitarian purposes in pioneer Alberta, Henry combined utility with aesthetics, leaning heavily on the side of the latter. As commonly happens, the two aligned. Throughout history, the beauty designed into a building to lend colour, texture, and warmth, often proved to be functional as well. Even when function isn't apparent, beauty still serves that universal need for things that are not strictly necessary. That which was not necessary was painstakingly worked into the holistic scheme that gradually emerged. The builder became the slave of the agenda, and the idea gradually unfolded into a tangible form, while he worked for her.

In the summer he worked for wages wherever he could. Some say that he once worked at the Bird's Eye Ranch—a cattle ranch near Cardston. But the present owners have no record of that, and no one can confirm or deny the claim.

Also, during the summer, he would order his building materials to have them by winter, when he could work full time on his house. By fall, Henry would have earned enough to pay for the supplies ordered during the summer. So, while the materials he ordered were nothing but the best, he always had sufficient earnings to settle his accounts before winter set in.

Henry bought much his building materials from Mayfare Lumber and Advanced Lumber Company in Lethbridge. Ed Cook, manager of Advanced Lumber, ordered and cut the hardwood panels for Henry and shipped bundles of wood and other materials to him. Some of the wood came from Italy and other parts of Europe. Stained glass, with swirls of brilliant colour, also came from Italy, where a special technique was used. Blown glass was spread over a sand base, resulting in one side being smooth and the other sand-pitted. The glass was expensive as were the other materials, but he willingly endured an ascetic existence for the woman he believed would one day occupy his house as his wife.

Henry would wait anxiously for his glass to arrive from Italy. At such times he would show extreme agitation. When it would finally arrive, he would carefully cut and shape the pieces into various geometric forms, based on the hexagon, and create more tiffany lamps and fixtures.

When Henry worked on his house, he became totally absorbed, regardless of the complexity or simplicity of the task. Whatever was done had to be done perfectly no matter how much time or effort it might take. For Henry, excellence was not an option, it was a need. It was one of the things that makes human beings human. He worked with hand tools, many of which he made himself. He made chisels of various sizes, angles and shapes.

During the long winters, when he had no other employment, Henry would sequester himself within his rock walls, warmed by the blaze of his fireplaces, and he would toil alone like a hermitic monk. But, on occasions, Charley Beck would drop by and help him make his honey-combed ceiling panels. Charley was about five-foot-seven inches tall and slight of build. He had dark hair and dark eyes. He probably became Henry's best friend, even though he was less than half Henry's age. He enjoyed his visits with Henry. There was always so much to learn from such a master craftsman. Charley's father, Robert, was an excellent carpenter and was teaching Charley the trade. Robert practiced conventional carpentry. Henry's techniques, on the other hand, were anything but conventional. He came from the European school which emphasized esthetics and creativity. His unorthodox methods drew Charley to Henry like a magnet, and Henry became his teacher, his mentor, his friend.

Using a miter box, Henry cut the small strips of solid oak to fit the intricate design of the paneling. He started the panels on oak veneer sheets onto which he nailed and glued the strips. He fashioned each panel integrally and then attached it to the walls and ceilings with more oak stripping. While thus engaged, Henry would talk about his fiancee. Sometimes he would say things that suggested that she wasn't going to come. Then he would fall silent, become pensive and refuse to talk about it anymore.

Henry had been out of work since the completion of the temple. This gave him time to work on his house, but he had no stable income. He earned some money by making and selling furniture.

Henry finished the dark oak room shortly after the completion of the temple. Several exotic woods were used, but mostly dark oak, used to frame the room's wall panels. It was a grand room, rich in somber tones like a Rembrant painting; like frozen baroque music. It could have been a setting for Edgar Allen Poe's *The Raven* and the lost Lenore. It was warm, but ominous. And the icy wind blowing, across the empty prairie, beat relentlessly upon the impenetrable edifice.

In the early twenties, electricity was a luxury in Cardston. On October 1, 1926, twenty-four-hour electrical service, except on Sunday afternoons, became available to Cardston residents. Those homes, wired for electricity, usually installed a single light, which hung from the ceiling of one room. Henry installed more than forty lights in the dark oak room. Along with his tiffany lamps, Henry installed indirect lighting behind cabinets and bookcases in such a way as to deliver a variegated glow through swirled stained glass doors.

Massive dark oak rocking chairs and straight-back chairs were randomly placed throughout the room. Henry made them all. The style was the same and somewhat puritanical with straight vertical struts attaching the wide chair arms and back to the seat. The rockers were perfectly balanced. They didn't look comfortable, but, they were. He made one of these rockers for Charley. It remains a prized possession of the family.

The last room Henry worked on was the Golden Oak room. He never finished it. It had a much lighter quality, but the style was similar to that of the dark oak room. While the dark room carried the somber tones of a Rembrant, the golden room played on the bright, airy gaiety of a Renoir. One stepped up four inches into the room through a door leading from the dark oak room. Large windows, six feet tall and four feet wide, with small panes, lined the south and west walls of the room, flooding it with light and giving the smooth panels the appearance of gold leaf. Henry built a cobblestone fireplace on the east wall. It is not known whether Henry installed stained-glass lamps in this room.

Although the ceilings and walls of the two rooms were finished with hard woods, Henry used fir for the floor. He designed hand made doors and windows, according to his own specifications that called for unusual proportions.

The original windows are especially noteworthy. Because windows tend to lose five to ten times more heat than do walls and ceilings, it is energy efficient to use windows sparingly where extremely cold weather prevails. On the other hand, windows can provide passive solar heating if planned and installed properly. And, who could argue against the value of natural light inundating a room or the view that it presents?

Henry used a special technique for making his own thermopanes—a process unheard of at the time. Each window contained two panes of glass separated by three-millimetre wide hardwood strips. He applied a mixture containing ammonia to the insides of the glass before sealing them. This created an inert gas trapped inside the space, providing very effective insulation. Where Henry learned this method of insulating glass is not known. He might have picked it up in Europe. Even today, windows insulated with an inert gas are not common. Most thermopane windows contain an empty air space between panes. Only the most advanced and expensive windows contain an inert gas like argon or krypton, the same gases used in electric bulbs and tubes that significantly reduces heat loss.

By facing his windows south, Henry added to the energy efficiency of his windows by taking advantage of the most direct and strongest rays of the sun during the day. Those windows facing westward caught the afternoon and evening sun. This arrangement supplies the house with a certain amount of free passive solar energy.

Henry built three unique fireplaces out of small cobblestones. He then finished them by staining the stones and covering them with beeswax. The beeswax eliminated the problem of soot sticking to the cobblestones.

The final addition to the house was a glass enclosed verandah that had its entrance on the east side and was tied into the original house. Henry used it as a green house. Cobblestone pillars supported it. These pillars still stand and serve the function for which they were originally designed.

Without a job, Henry apparently began to run short of money. At the same time he was buying more building materials, and he also started to buy expensive furnishings for the house, something he never did before. He had always made his own furniture. He appeared to be in a hurry to get things done. He worked at a more feverish pace, and began contracting debts. That was not like him. His finances might have become critical at this point had not a lucky break occurred. Plans for the building of a hotel in Waterton National Park, a short distance from Cardston, were being rumored. If true, it would mean a job and a steady income for Henry.

5. The Recluse

IN August 1903, Edward J. Wood became president of the Alberta stake. As president he supervised the building of the Alberta temple. When it was completed he became its president—a position he held until 1948. He was one of the most influential men in southern Alberta, liked and respected by Mormons and non-Mormons alike. And, he, in turn, loved people.

In spite of Henry Hoet's eccentricities, Edward Wood liked and respected him. He liked him as a cultured and intelligent man; he liked him as a fine and gifted artist.

Most of the community treated Henry well and respected his privacy. Historically, Mormons commonly displayed tolerance and generosity. They knew too well what it was like to experience intolerance. They were among the only settlers in western United States that consistently maintained friendly relations with the Indians. It was easier to accept them on their own terms than to fight them. But, there remained some in the community who didn't feel comfortable with Henry, the quiet bachelor with the big dog.

The opposite was true of Edward Wood. On frequent occasions he encouraged his son, Forest, to visit Henry. He believed that Henry could teach

Forest a lot. "Learn all you can from Henry," advised his father.

Forest did visit Henry, and he walked into a world of unusual richness—a world of golden and dark mahogany panels, built-in bookcases, rare and wonderful stained glass, set in numerous tiffany lamps with small scraps of exotic wood. Some of the honeycombed panels required as many as sixty-one intricately carved and fitted pieces of wood. He talked at length with the kindly wizard.

Forest found nothing strange or frightening about Henry. His dress and personal appearance was often unkept, but that was not uncommon in a frontier community. He was too occupied with his work to allow himself the luxury of good grooming. Besides, he had no place to go and no one to impress. He did, however, keep the house neat and clean.

"Henry was a very friendly man," said Forest. "He always welcomed me. He showed me his work and explained it to me. He would take time off to show me around. I had nice visits with him. I was nineteen. He was a conversationalist. He said he liked to build things: tables, chairs, china cabinets. Henry never bothered anybody; it seemed others bothered him."

He made most of his own furniture. Every joint fit perfectly. He even made his own tools. If he needed a special tool, he made it. Many people in Cardston and the surrounding area own and proudly display furniture and other items made by Henry.

"He was a very efficient cabinet maker," continued Forest. "He made my father a large China Cabinet and I now have it. He also designed in gold."

He seemed to do everything in an unorthodox way. Forest said that he applied the finishing to much of his work with his fingers rather than with a brush or applicator.

Some of the younger kids in the area were afraid of Henry and his dog. A lack of communications developed between him and some of the kids. It all came about as a result of the best swimming hole being located about one hundred metres from Henry's house. For reasons unknown, Henry didn't like the kids swimming in the creek so near his house, and he was adamant that they not cross his property while going to or coming from the swimming hole.

Lyman Jacobs used to swim in the creek as a kid. "If the kids came down along the creek near his house," said Lyman, "Henry would come out with his big dog and make sure the kids left. He was an arch-enemy of out door life," Lyman said, referring to the kids.

Henry was not totally to blame for the tension that existed between him and the kids. Because Henry was different, some of the kids liked to play jokes on him. One of their favorites was knocking on his door, and then running away. At times they would shout abuse at him.

Henry did not limit his territorial imperative to kids; it extended to other living things as well.

Joseph C. Shaw lived in Cardston and raised his family there. His work on the Alberta Temple brought him in close contact with Henry, and he became very fond of him. His daughter Laurene said that he often spoke well of Henry and told humorous stories about him.

One story told of Henry being awakened early one morning with a rapid tapping on his roof. He jumped up, grabbed his rifle and ran outside to investigate. On his roof, three woodpeckers were hammering on his shingles. Henry immediately commenced firing at the startled feathery foes that fluttered away in surprised frustration.

"I shooted at them!" He exclaimed to Shaw, miming the experience with flailing arms where words failed.

Another Cardston resident, who was a young boy when Henry was building his house, said that his only memory of him was: "He did not like them [the kids] on his property and would chase them away whenever they took a short cut from the creek."

Lyman admitted that it was probably the dog that spooked the kids and gave them the impression that Henry was a mean and cantankerous hermit. But the dog never displayed aggression toward anyone. It never even barked much less growled or attacked anyone. It was content to remain at Henry's side. In the house it would lie beside Henry's rocking chair in front of the fireplace, his head resting lazily between his outstretched paws. Henry and his dog were inseparable. He took the dog with him wherever he went.

Cardston was a quiet prairie town with not a lot of exciting things for kids to do. They had much time for imaginative speculation. Henry, because he was different, became a special target for such speculation. He appeared particularly odd to kids, when they walked by his house early in the morning on their frequent hunting, fishing, or berry-picking expeditions, to see his lights streaming through his windows. They could see him bowed and lost in his work, like a magician conjuring up eerie and frightful things from some nether world, while the rest of the town slumbered in peace. This would start them thinking about what sorcery the "mad genius" was up to in his private temple.

Hope Salway, Harold's sister, confirmed that many of the kids were afraid of Henry, but she wasn't. She recalled one incident when she and some of her friends went picking rose hips close to Henry's house. He came out to see what they were doing. She told him and explained about all the good things that could be made from rose hips—tea, syrup, jam. Henry listened to this nine or ten-year-old girl and then disappeared into the house. When he reappeared, he too had a container, and he quietly joined the kids picking rose hips. At other times the kids picked Saskatoon berries behind Henry's house. He never bothered them when they were so occupied.

Others in the community worried about Henry's, poor eating habits and the way in which he neglected his health. Several ladies in Cardston would occasionally send him freshly baked bread, pies, or something left over from their meal.

Minnie Beck often sent Henry food with her young children. Ethel Beck was only five or six at the time, but she remembered that Henry would often appear not to understand.

"His mind would seem to be elsewhere," said Ethel. "Then it would clear. He would accept the food graciously and say to us: 'Tell your mother thank you. But, I can manage. I can manage.' He was a very proud man and didn't want to accept charity.

"'I know your mother wants you to go right back home,' Henry would insist. 'We don't want you to get lost.'"

Ethel remembers being very curious about what was behind the door. She tried, without success, to steal a few glances around the kindly man, who barred the way into a world she could only imagine—a world of brilliant light and colour.

She almost got into the house on another occasion, when she and one of her brother's took Henry a loaf of freshly baked bread. Henry invited them in. Her brother accepted the invitation and entered, but Ethel was too afraid of the dog to go in with her brother. She was left waiting outside, regretting her unfounded fears.

She would have to wait several years before she could experience the full magic of what lay behind the enchanted door, but by then the wizard was gone.

The Salways lived across the street from Henry in an old log house. Harold Salway was a young boy at the time, but he remembers that, "time meant nothing to him [Henry]. He would work until he needed to eat and stop long enough to eat food that did not require much cooking. Honey, peanut butter, bread and jam with coffee made up the bulk of his diet. Having eaten he would get right back to work."

Harold likes to recall the times when Henry was away working on the Prince of Wales Hotel at Waterton National Park. An adventuresome fourteen year old boy with an insatiable curiosity, he discovered a small opening in the foundation of Henry's house. It led to a small basement or cellar under the kitchen. From there, he had easy access to the rest of the house. What he beheld was something out of the

Arabian Nights. Like a Moorish palace, massive rock walls, covered with amazing panels of brilliant design, bedazzled the boy, accustomed to the crowded, but cozy gloom of a rustic log cabin. The many shapes and swirling colors of the stained glass in the Tiffany lamps mesmerized him.

"It was a whole new world of wonder to me," said Harold. "Henry had built many fine oak chairs, including several perfectly balanced rocking chairs. I also discovered that he loved to read. He had subscribed to the *Little Big Books*. These were small paperback books condensed from the original works, somewhat in the manner of the Readers Digest. Each book was about 3 inches by four inches and about a quarter of an inch thick. They were like miniature encyclopedias without pictures covering every subject a young boy could imagine.

"I loved them and spent many hours in Henry's rocking chair reading these little books. It seemed there were hundreds of them."

Henry may have used these books to help him improve his English. He was an avid reader. He would read anything. Charley's father, Robert, would take Henry his newspapers after he had finished reading them.

Like some others in the community, Gene Salway considered Henry deranged. Like his brother, Gene also occasionally broke into Henry's house, but his interests didn't include the books that had so captivated his brother. Gene's forte was exploration, and the Rock House became a sanctum to examine from top to bottom, stem to stern. Gene was mostly interested in the attic. Here he found a vast assortment of interesting items, including a mattress covered with fish hooks like a pin cushion, and, in one corner, a life-sized doll or mannequin.

Gene recalled Henry's one indulgence. He liked tobacco. But even with this he was stoically frugal. After chewing his tobacco, he would allow the wad to dry. Then he would pulverize it and roll it into cigarettes.

He wasted nothing, including time. The sooner he finished building his house, the sooner his fiancee would join him. But he had to be meticulous—she deserved only the best. When he became too tired to work, he would sit in one of his rocking chairs and allow himself a moment to sleep and dream. On waking, he would continue working. "Day or night meant nothing to him."

While most agreed that Henry was eccentric, most of the community believed he was harmless. He was never aggressive; just the opposite—quiet, shy, withdrawn.

Perhaps he was a loner because he knew he spoke poor English, and that may have embarrassed him. He was a romantic, and perhaps he really believed that the magic he could perform with his skilled hands would be the same magic that would transform his dreams for a wife into reality. Perhaps he did chase kids off his property, and perhaps he did this because he didn't want them to get hurt. His property was a construction site, and a construction site is not a safe place for kids to play.

On the other hand, anyone visiting Henry was welcomed and treated with good manners and respect. Henry's dog might look ferocious to the kids, but, in fact, it wasn't. Henry neglected his health, but is that uncommon among bachelors? He was obsessed with work, but should not that have been considered a virtue, especially in a Mormon community where there are so many examples of hard workers? He didn't take part in community events, but then, did anyone ever invite him to do so? The Mormons are friendly people, but they do make up a quasi closed society, and they associate more with fellow Mormons than they do with those outside the faith. Henry was a Catholic, and, in the community in which he lived, he was odd.

6. Prince of Wales Hotel

In March 1926, Louis Hill, president of the Great Northern Railway and son of James Hill, its founder, announced his plan to build a hotel at Waterton Lakes National Park, situated on the eastern slopes of the Rocky Mountains in southwestern Alberta, just north of the U.S. border. Waterton Lakes National Park, named after Charles Waterton, an eccentric English naturalist, gained its status by act of parliament on June 8, 1911. The proposed hotel would be named the Prince of Wales Hotel after the Duke of Windsor who briefly became Edward the VIII in 1936. He abdicated the throne that year to marry the American actress and divorcee, Wallis Warfield Simpson.

Louis Hill conceived the idea of establishing bus tours from Glacier National Park in Montana to Banff and Jasper in Alberta. Waterton Lakes, which was not served by a rail line, would benefit by having a bus route through the lake region. With quality accommodations, Waterton National Park would provide an excellent stopover for the anticipated multitude of tourists that would be attracted by some of the most beautiful and pristine scenery in the world.

In the fall of 1925, Hill visited Waterton and liked what he saw. On a wind swept knoll overlooking Middle and Upper Waterton Lakes, Hill decided that this would be the perfect place to build his hotel. The storybook scene nestles three Waterton lakes between two mountain ranges. Mount Blakiston is the most imposing mountain in view of the site. It rises to an altitude of 2,926 metres. It is named after Lieutenant Thomas Blakiston who explored the mountain regions in the summer of 1858 for the British government to determine the feasibility of building a railroad across Canada. The Waterton River and several brooks feed the lakes.

Hill set up a company and called it the Canadian Rockies Hotel Co. Ltd. Then he began negotiations with the Canadian government.

Impressed with Hill's proposal, the government granted the Great Northern Railway a forty-two-year lease on ten acres of the Hill on which the hotel would be built. Hill estimated the cost of construction at $250,000.

In March 1926, Hill officially announced the Railway's intention to build the hotel. He had traveled extensively in Switzerland and had become fascinated with the chalets that dotted the Swiss landscape. He admired the unconcealed structural members and wide overhang. It would be the type of architecture that would compliment and blend with the Waterton National Park environment. He immediately commissioned a Swiss architect to draw up the plans.

Hill's next task was to find a contractor. He wanted one already established close to the site. He found one in Cardston. Oland and Scott Construction Company of Cardston was a small company and unknown outside of southern Alberta. The partners, forty-one-year-old Doug Oland and thirty-eight-year-old Jim Scott, were dreamers, filled with optimism, but they knew how to be aggressive when necessary. This was especially true of Oland. He was six feet tall and husky, mild-mannered, and jovial. Scott projected a more retiring personality. Both were friendly and well liked by the people in the area, and that gave them influence.

When the Great Northern sent their engineers to Waterton to survey the site on which the hotel would be built, Oland became acquainted with the head engineer, Floyd Parker. After talking to him, Oland decided to try to land the job of building the hotel for his company. He wrote the Great Northern offices in St. Paul, Minnesota, giving as references the manager of the Bank of Montreal and the mayor of Cardston. Both were friends of his.

It was a long shot, and it is doubtful that either of the partners really expected to get the job, but, investigations made by the Great Northern into the reputation of the company must have been positive. The company held very few assets and had little money, but it was well known that the company had always paid its commitments, even when the partners, themselves, had to go short. Still, it must have been a pleasant surprise when they received a letter from the Great Northern's chief engineer asking them to make a proposal.

Oland and Scott put their heads together and began crunching numbers. They had no idea of the cost of building such a grand hotel. The job was too big, and it seemed to be out of their ballpark. Both recognized that they would never be able to come up with the financing, so they offered to do the job on a cost plus five percent arrangement.

A reply from St. Paul soon followed. Conditions were laid out. Oland and Scott would have to furnish all the construction equipment, establish a camp, and feed and house the construction crew at no cost to the railroad. The Great Northern would pay for the building of the bunk houses and other utility buildings necessary for the camp.

Under these conditions Oland and Scott upped their bid to cost plus six-and-one-half percent. This turned out to be exactly the amount the Great Northern paid for the building of the Glacier park hotels. Oland then negotiated a loan from a bank in Cardston for Twelve thousand dollars—an amount considered to be the minimum necessary to start construction.

In a short time and without warning, the Great Northern's chief engineer arrived in Cardston. He came prepared to offer Oland and Scott a contract. All he wanted was assurance that the contractors would be able to finance the start of the job. Oland took the chief engineer to the bank for that assurance. The manager wasn't in. He had gone on holidays without informing the man left in charge about the loan that had already been approved by the Calgary superintendent. A call to Calgary disclosed that the superintendent too was on holiday and could not be found. Oland envisioned his plum contract evaporating before his eyes in a series of fluke incidents.

In desperation he drove to Lethbridge, hoping to contract a loan there. The bank manager received Oland with little sympathy. Oland left the bank with only a promise that the bank manager would meet him in Cardston on the following day and further discuss the matter, but Oland received little encouragement.

In a last despairing effort to keep the contract that would greatly enhance his reputation, he turned to an old friend. Morris Stoltze owned a number of lumber yards in southern Alberta. He was not eager to lend Oland $12,000, a sizable amount in the mid-1920s, but he did agree to make the loan if all else failed. And it did.

The next morning, the bank manager met with Oland and the engineer. The manager told them that the loan would be approved, but, according to regulations, the bank would have to take an assignment of the contract.

The chief engineer bristled. A moment of uncomfortable silence passed. Then he informed the bank manager that he had come to Cardston, prepared to give Oland and Scott the contract, mainly on the recommendation of the bank. The railroad was prepared to lend Oland and Scott up to forty thousand dollars a month and were asking the bank to advance twelve thousand. He told the manager that any money his company would be sending would go directly to Oland and Scott and not the bank. Then he added:

"There is one thing wrong with your bank managers. You are too cold blooded!"

They got up and left.

In his Memoirs, Oland wrote: "I want to say here that he [the engineer] was one of the finest and fairest men it has been my experience to deal with."

Forced to play his last card, Oland took the engineer to the Advanced Lumber Company. Stoltze was in his office awaiting them. Without hesitation, the loan was made and Oland and Scott Construction

Company was awarded the contract. And a gem of a contract it was. It was specifically designed to help Oland and Scott get over the many financial hurdles faced by most companies. Because they were not strong financially, the Great Northern helped pave the way for the fledgling company.

All parties signed the contract, and work began on July 12, 1926. Oland arrived at Waterton with a small crew. Henry Hoet was included. Henry had established a reputation for excellent workmanship, and Oland wanted him with his celebrated skills to do the finishing work on the hotel. The crew expanded to sixty men by fall.

Henry needed the job. It had been a long dry spell since he had steady employment. His resources had dwindled, and he began borrowing money. At first he did not want to leave working on his house, and he did so reluctantly. But, his need for funds overcame his reluctance.

Henry came to enjoy working on the hotel. To be paid for doing what he passionately loved, and would gladly do for nothing, was a fortunate circumstance.

As the hotel took form, it more and more reminded him of the chalets of Europe. The memory filled him with a sweet nostalgia, but he didn't talk about it except on rare occasions with Charley. But, then he would catch himself and fall silent.

Henry loved the natural environment, and he must have often dreamt of someday taking his fiancee to this wild and beautiful land.

Henry rode to Waterton with his two friends, Charley and Robert in Robert's Model T Ford. Robert Beck was admired as an excellent carpenter. He worked in construction most of his life and was often away from home. He was a stern man who stood six foot-one and was of medium build. When at home, he was the unquestionable head of his household. His daughter Ethel described him as a man who never had to tell you to do something twice. But as stern as he was, he always treated Henry with respect and generosity.

Charley did not take after his dad. His nature was more delicate, probably because he suffered from asthma. In spite of his health, he became a good carpenter, but his work capacity was limited, because of his delicate health.

Henry's dog rode in a utility box, like a pick-up bed, attached to the back of the car. Henry shared one of the cabins, supplied for the workers, with the Becks. So, as Henry bounced about in the Model T Ford on the twenty-five kilometre dusty and later muddy road to Waterton National Park, he devoured the spectacular scenery. The grass-covered rolling hills of the prairies suddenly, within a kilometre, transformed into a rugged mountainous terrain, where snow-clad peaks soured to heights of nearly 3,000 metres. Indians knew this place as the "Land of Shining Mountains."

Within the park boundaries, there breathed a land pulsating and teeming with life. Mule and white-tail deer scanned the land with dark liquid eyes and nervous twitching. Mountain goats, with long sad faces, perched dangerously on rock ledges, high above ground level. Bighorn sheep with horns like cornucopia; the bounding antelope on springed hooves; the slinking coyote and its arched jump on hapless prey; the elk in the late fall, bugling eerily during rutting season; the lovable but ungainly moose slurping green slime while standing knee high in a pond, his bulbous proboscis submerged to his eyeballs; the myriad squirrels and chipmunks chattering angrily at trespassers; and the other fifty-seven species of mammals that lived in the park practiced and repeated their age old antics.

Nature brought its pallet and paintbrush to this enchanted land and distributed liberally more than nine hundred species of flora. They grew in profusion in the valleys and on the mountain slopes. There were crimson splashes of the Indian paint brush; the golden yellow buttercup; lupine with its purple, spiked florescence; the golden aster; the purple Jones' columbine, swaying on its stems like silken vertebrae; the glacier lily bowing its yellow petals, shaped like a jester's hat; the ubiquitous wild rose.

They chugged past fields of bear grass—a species found in Waterton and in no other national park. Its flowering stalks rose more than a meter in the air, showing off clusters of creamy white flowers. Saskatoon berries and chokecherries flourished on the lower mountain slopes.

The area is home to more than two hundred thirty-four species of birds, including the daring gray jay, better known as the camp robber or whiskey jack, and his cousin, the equally bold Steller Jay, donned in a rich blue to blue-black coat. It was named after the German naturalist, George W. Steller. He discovered the bird while a member of the Vitus Bering expedition, which discovered Alaska in the early eighteenth century. In the fall, vast numbers of Waterfowl, the itinerants of the park, appeared on the lakes and ponds to rest awhile before resuming their flight south. Grouped according to kind, like members of exclusive clubs, they included mallards, ruddy ducks, golden eyes, buffleheads, widgeons, Canada geese, grebes, and tundra swans, to mention but a few.

Peering down from dead branches, perched the regal bald eagle.

Into view came the quaint town of Waterton. It was already a well-established community when construction crews started pouring into the area. Log cabins, field stone and shingle-sided cottages dominated the town and overlooked one of the lakes. There were government buildings and a police station. A post office, hotel, furnished cottage rentals, a restaurant, rooming house, dance hall, and two general stores completed the portrait of the scenic town.

These were the sights to which Henry became accustomed during the time he worked at Waterton. He and the Becks roomed at Waterton during the week and came home to Cardston on the weekends. This period of Henry's life was short but rich in the beauty of nature and in the beauty of his own creation that was nearing completion.

Oland's first task at Waterton, was to build a small residence for himself on the site of the construction camp, so that he could stay at Waterton and devote all his time to the job. The park paid for his house. During the first six months, Oland worked sixteen hours a day to get things organized his way.

The summer days were kind. Gentle breezes bathed the area in tenderness. During warm, dry weather, the crew grew to about sixty men. Most of them came from the Cardston area. The work progressed according to schedule until the bad weather struck. It started to rain in August. Soon the dirt road from the rail head at Cardston became a muddy, mucilaginous gumbo, impassable for big trucks. The only trucks that had any hope of getting through were the smaller ones, ton-and-a-half and less. Soon, not even these could get through, and teams of horses had to be pressed into service. The weather and the roads continued to worsen. Work slowed to a crawl, and Oland was forced to lay off twenty-five men.

Waterton's climate is capricious at best, violent and nasty at worst, but the terrain is always wildly beautiful. Days without wind are few. It is a constant that one grows used to. Average breezes are thirty-two kilometres per hour, but gale force winds can approach one hundred sixty kilometres per hour, producing screaming howls through mountains and trees, confirming that beauty exacts its price. On the other hand, bitter cold and deep snow can be whisked away by a dry westerly Chinook wind within moments.

Because of bad weather and bad roads, transportation costs soared. During the early part of construction it cost four dollars a thousand board feet of lumber hauled from Cardston, but that increased to twenty-four dollars a thousand delivered, as the roads progressively deteriorated. All materials had to come over what became a quagmire—one hundred carloads of lumber, about fifty carloads of plaster, and almost a hundred carloads of plumbing and heating supplies, and numerous other materials.

Freight started pouring in to the rail depot at Cardston faster than it could be conveyed to Waterton. Crews built large storage sheds at Waterton and Cardston to take the flood of material.

Reliable men were hired for the sole purpose of receiving and checking out goods.

Hill took off on a shopping frenzy for the Great Northern. He bought hundreds of thousands of dollars worth of material in Vancouver that he shipped to Cardston by way of the United States. Oland and Scott often knew nothing of the material being shipped until it suddenly appeared in Cardston or Waterton.

In spite of transportation problems, construction progressed according to schedule. Then Hill began making changes with agonizing regularity. Twice a week mail came to Waterton. Nearly that often, Hill ordered changes to the construction plans.

He traipsed through France and Switzerland, drawing a throng of photographers in his wake. Every time something struck his eye, he would have pictures taken. These would be sent to the architect with orders to make the desired changes. The hotel became Hill's hobby. He studied French and Swiss chalets with intense interest. He took what he considered the best and ordered changes be made accordingly. As a result, much of the completed structure was built as many as four times.

Early in December the crew had completely framed the walls and roof of the seven-story structure. All had to be torn down to the first floor to accommodate Hill's changes. Then the snow fell. More than thirty-five centimetres fell, and more than fifty thousand dollars was spent shoveling it. Every time it snowed, carpenters were laid off, and a crew of labourers hired to clear the building of snow.

The first stage of construction consisted mainly of rough carpentry. This was not Henry's forte, and he was not good at it. Neither was he arrogant. He knew his weaknesses and was willing to listen, watch, and learn from others, but, when there was finishing work to be done, Henry was called upon. His most notable work included the making of the stained glass ceiling lamps, similar to those he made for his house.

Years later, when the Prince of Wales Hotel was being renovated, workmen removed Henry's lamps, piled them up behind the hotel, and set them ablaze. Don Remington, a wealthy rancher and founder of the Remington Carriage Museum in Cardston, heard about the lamps being dismantled. He hurried to Waterton to buy them but arrived too late. All that remained was glowing ashes and melted glass.

Charley and Henry usually worked together. "He was slow," said Charley, "because he was a perfectionist. Everything had to be perfect."

His slow deliberate accuracy possessed a kind of rhythm—a ballet of eyes and hands. There was a concentrated intensity on the task at hand, totally isolated from all other things.

When in the presence of others, he was also fussy about his own personal neatness. His manners were excellent. He would never think of entering a place without removing his hat. His behavior and general mien resembled that of an aristocrat, which led some to believe that he came from an upper class family, and, for some reason, was disowned.

Some of the crew took pleasure in teasing Henry about his phantom girl friend. This was done light-heartedly, and no ill will was intended. Henry ignored the teasing. He went about his work, lost in his own thoughts. But, his mental state began to gradually change as a terrible illness began eating away at him.

By mid January, those laid off earlier were rehired, and the crew again numbered sixty. For the second time, they completed the framing and firmly secured it to the foundation. But, not firmly enough.

One night in February, gale-force winds viciously assaulted the skeletal framework. Throughout the night, gust after gust battered the exposed structure, threatening to collapse it. Creaking timbers groaned throughout the night. With the dawn, the wind eased. The structure remained standing, but it didn't totally escape the night's fury. The relentless winds had pushed the framework twenty-three centimetres off its foundation. Oland surveyed the damage with a sinking heart. How does one move a fifty meter high skeleton of a building back to its proper place?

Oland decided to try horse-powered winches. Little by little the building yielded to the brute power of the horses and winches. There were tense moments. The structure creaked in protest, but, at last, it stood unscathed on its foundation, as close to square as it was going to get. It remains to this day slightly off base.

Spring dawned with the omnipresent sound of trickling water and the drip of melting icicles. Snow banks melted into small creeks, and the swollen mountain streams began to cascade down into the valleys in a symphonic crescendo.

Again the roads were soft. The Model T skidded and slid over the road carrying Henry and the Becks to Waterton. It was like driving on Crisco. Over the sound of the chugging engine and the spin of tires came the sound of birds, accompanied by water music in a rite of spring—in a celebration of life.

It was early April. Oland received word from St. Paul that the Great Northern would have to delay the hotel's opening until the following year because of the harsh weather and the many plan changes. The hotel had already accepted reservations for the summer, but they would have to be canceled.

Oland replied at once. He wrote of his progress and that he already had the roof on. He assured them that, if they could guarantee him delivery of needed materials on time, and if they would quit changing plans, he would give them their hotel on time. They trusted his word, and Oland increased his work force to one hundred twenty-five men.

Much work still had to be done. A power house had to be built and a sewer system installed, including a septic tank almost one hundred feet long. Crews were put to work building a pumping station and a large laundry under the same roof as the boilers and diesel engines. The engines were used to generate electricity. Waterton was not serviced for electricity at the time. The crew also made the frames for the lobby lanterns. To add to the stress of his tight timetable, Oland was now asked to build ninety bedroom suits.

His congenial nature began to show signs of strain. His answering letter stated sharply "I would have been pleased to get this order the fall before as it would have enabled me to build a rough shed and keep my good carpenters busy during those many days it was impossible to work outside."

He further explained that, at this late date, it would be impossible to give them a hotel and furniture too. He suggested that he go to Calgary to see if he could sub contract the job out. Authorization was given, and Oland found a firm that agreed to supply the furniture.

As soon as one brush fire was doused another seemed to ignite. In May, two large boilers arrived by rail at Pincher Creek, fifty-nine kilometres north of Waterton. Spring runoff had turned the road to mush. There was no way to transport the boilers with the road in that condition. It seemed to Oland, that all of nature had joined forces to militate against the opening of the hotel. Then, on May 27, the temperature dropped and a heavy snow blanketed the area. That was the break Oland needed. The boilers were loaded on two sleds to which thirty horses were harnessed. Two days later, the boilers appeared in Waterton. Their average speed was a little over a kilometre per hour.

Two days before the scheduled opening of the hotel, Captain R. Stanley Harrison, manager of the new Hotel, approached Oland. He was disturbed and close to tears. Not one bedstead had arrived.

Oland made a quick mental calculation and then promised Harrison that, if he could supply the necessary materials, his workmen, who now numbered 230, would give them a bedstead in every room before opening day. Harrison didn't believe that possible, but he had no alternative but to trust Oland to deliver. And he did. His carpenters produced the one hundred eighty beds.

"Springs and mattresses were placed on the beds and covered with Hudson Bay Blankets. There was a bed in every bed room by 6 PM," wrote Oland in his Memoirs.

On July 25, the Prince of Wales Hotel officially opened, and guests began to arrive. The seven-story chalet was a work of art in an environment unparalleled for its pristine beauty. All woodwork was intricately fitted and pegged. No nails were used.

Oland had carried out his promise, in the face of severe obstacles. The Great Northern had their hotel on July 16, fifteen days after the date specified on the contract.

7. Loila

HENRY'S job at Waterton kept him away from his house more than he would have liked. He was eager to finish his house. It seemed as though he was racing with time. When he was home, he worked like a demon, neglecting his health, even more now than he had previously. A sort of intoxication came over him; work developed into an orgy.

His health continued to deteriorate, and he developed large carbuncles. One on the back of his neck was particularly painful. Eva Salway, wife of Alfred, Cardston's barber, gardener and spectacle salesman, was a gentle, pious lady who loved writing poetry, much of which she had published. She was also an amateur dramatist.

She always gave Henry a warm welcome when he came to visit. She would lay aside her hooked rug, or whatever else she was working on, to apply hot poultices to Henry's neck to soften the aching carbuncle before lancing it. She made her poultices with stale, wet bread wrapped in hot towels.

She would scold Henry for neglecting and abusing himself. He'd agree and shrug his shoulders. Eva knew she wasted her breath. She'd shake her head sadly as he'd close the door behind him and return to his endless labour across the street.

Charley began visiting Henry more often. But the only way to visit Henry was to work with him. Henry wouldn't stop working simply because he had a visitor. Charley didn't mind. He rather enjoyed helping Henry put together his ceiling panels.

It was around this time (1926-1927) that Charley detected a strangeness in Henry that he hadn't noticed before.

Henry continued to talk about his fiancee as before, but doubt seemed to have crept into his mind. Words would slip out suggesting that maybe she wasn't going to come and join him after all. Then, as usual, he would slip into silence and begin muttering under his breath. Sometimes he would seem disoriented and confused, but Charley believed the problem was the result of little food and sleep. This is why both Robert and Charley often asked Mrs. Beck to prepare extra food for Henry.

Charley began to doubt that Henry's alleged fiancee would ever come to Canada. From bits and pieces of conversation, he began to wonder if she hadn't long ago married some one else. He even began to question her very existence. Could she be merely a figment of his imagination? Maybe Henry made himself believe that if he completed the house, she would come.

"She will change her mind," Henry often mumbled.

Charley never saw any letters. He never saw Henry writing any or receiving any. He never saw anything in the house that looked as if it came from Belgium. He did, however, see some strange aberrations in Henry's behavior that he couldn't understand. That concerned him.

At other times Henry would be his old self, taciturn and busy, but keenly aware of his surroundings.

Henry Hoet in his unfinished Dark Oak Room

One of the many China Cabinets built by Henry Hoet.
This one is now owned by Forest Wood

Prince of Wales Hotel soon after it was built.
(Glenbow Archives, Calgary, Alberta NB-32-7 and NB 32-8

The Mormon Temple as it appears today

Two views of the Dark Oak Room, featuring stained glass lighting fixtures

Two views of the Golden Oak Room as it appears today (Photos by James Musson)

Loila Williams (1906-1949) from her *Journal*,
complements of Laura L. Barrus

Cobblestone Manor as it appeared in 1928. (Glenbow Archives, Calgary, Alberta ND-27-38

Present owners of Cobblestone Manor, Ed Flickinger (far left) and Arlene Flickinger (standing third from left) and part of their extended family.

As the house neared completion, Henry began to get curious visitors. Few people then living in southern Alberta had ever seen a house as grand as his.

Harold Salway took the direct approach and simply broke in through the cellar and made himself at home when Henry was away at Waterton. The young girls in the area took another approach. They simply imposed on his privacy and spent enjoyable hours watching him convert the golden oak room into a chamber equal to a tsar's drawing room.

Among his visitors were Rojanea Jacobs and Anne Leishman. Both girls were about ten-or-eleven-years-old. They loved to visit Henry and watch him perform his magic. Rojanea was shy and preferred to stand back and watch in wonderment, but Anne was bold and brazen and liked to clown. She was a "big tease," said Rojanea, "and would threaten Henry, as he stood on his stool carefully attaching his honeycombed panels to the ceiling, that if he wasn't good, Santa Clause would place a big lump of coal in his stocking on Christmas Eve." Henry never teased in return. He didn't have a light side. The best one could get out of him was a kindly and patronizing smile. It, however, seemed obvious that he enjoyed their company. He never told them to leave.

Anne was a frequent visitor. She had no fear of Henry. On one of her visits, Henry gave her and her friend Hope Salway a personally conducted tour of the Rock House. It dazzled them.

Among Henry's earliest visitors was Pearl Duce and her sister. As teenagers they would walk by the house on their way home from school and curiously peer in at Henry while he worked. That was around 1920.

Pearl left Cardston to attend Normal School in Calgary, where she earned her teaching certificate. She taught in a couple of small country schools before landing a job in the Cardston Public School in 1924, where she taught for a couple of years. She never lost her curiosity in Henry's house, and she watched its progress with great interest.

A rumor started circulating that Henry was building the house for Pearl. Even in her later years, friends and relatives would tease her about that. She never denied the rumor, but would smile coyly when teased about it.

Henry seemed to be trying desperately to cling to the fading belief that his fiancee would soon join him, but the increasingly apparent futility of his endeavors was almost more than he could bear. Gradually, little by little, his fantasies began to wan and then shift. It began when he became aware of a young lady that seemed to be taking a special interest in his house. He was struck by her resemblance to his sweetheart in Belgium. There grew a sweet sickness that radiated around his heart. There appeared a sense of daji vous, an awareness that he had experienced such feelings before, somewhere in the receding light of a distant past. A new dream arose and he longed to leave this place in his mind and go to the very margins of awareness to clear a new place.

Her name was Loila Williams. She became a school teacher and taught in a number of small schools throughout the district. She was also the daughter of one of Cardston's founding fathers, Sterling Williams. He was the stepson of Ora Card and the grandson of Brigham Young. At age sixteen, he drove one of the first wagons into Cardston. He had traveled from Utah with his mother Zina, known in the community as aunt Zina. Since then he had done very well for himself. He became well educated, having attended Brigham Young Academy before coming to Canada. Later he returned to Utah and completed a two-year business course. He then entered Brandon University in Manitoba, where he received a scholarship and graduated with a silver medal, the highest award for scholastic excellence given by the university then. He became the first Mormon to receive a Bachelor of Arts degree from a western Canadian University. Returning home, he served as a teacher and principal in the Cardston Public School System. He later became a successful businessman. From the time he first arrived in Cardston, he held responsible church offices. A pillar of Cardston society, this versatile and venerable man was a pioneer, homesteader, rancher and stockman, educator, banker, businessman, and churchman, and Loila's father.

Like him, Loila was also versatile. Having come from a family of high achievers, she too reached high. When she was in grade 11, her 1922 school yearbook, *Hi Lights*, characterized her by the phrase: "High are thy thoughts."

She was a lovely, slender girl and wore her hair cropped somewhat in the flapper style. Her smile was gentle and calming. One was at ease with her. Her eyes were almond-shaped and conveyed a soft and amiable nature with a dash of mischief and mystery. At home and among those with whom she was close, she demonstrated a high degree of individuality and stubbornness. She was the only girl among four boys in the family. Often, they teased her unmercifully, but they always showed her every affection. They took her every place. She was adventurous and a willing conspirator in banter and kidding. Yet, outside her accustomed circle, she was shy and retiring, and delicate health often curbed her otherwise active life.

Loila developed an interest in art in grade school. She entered two art contests, one in Lethbridge and one in Calgary, and won both. When presented with five-dollar and ten-dollar prizes respectively, no one was more proud of her than her Dad. This delighted and encouraged Loila, because she was very close to him.

Because of poor health, she decided to take her grade twelve in two years, even though she usually did well in school. Her best subjects were science, math, history and art. She also liked to take part in public speaking contests and drama.

Perhaps she used her health as a ploy. What she really wanted was more time. Her family was planning to remodel their home, and Loila, with her flair for art, wanted to help. She ended up doing most of the finishing wood work. This is probably when she started going over to Henry's house. He certainly would have been an excellent source of information, and she could get some great remodeling ideas.

Having a kind and friendly disposition, Loila probably befriended Henry and found an artistic soul-mate. As they both possessed timid and retiring personalities, it would have been natural for them to tacitly share their interests. Henry would have taken great pleasure in showing her the workmanship in his house.

She graduated from High School in 1925, and enrolled in Calgary Normal School. It was her first time away from home. She lived in a rooming house with other girls and experienced more freedom than she ever had. She flourished socially, dating and going to dances and other social events. She also took part in a number of hikes throughout the surrounding area. Along with her required courses, she enrolled and completed a course in industrial arts. After thirty-six weeks she obtained a Grade "B" teaching certificate in physical education and obtained her first teaching job in Cardston. From then on her teaching career had many interruptions. She only taught for five years between 1926 and 1940. There were other interests to explore. Art was among them.

Her interest in art motivated Loila to occasionally visit the Rock House to see how Henry's work was progressing. She liked his work and knew good art when she saw it. She could recognize genius as well. So, it's no wonder she enjoyed watching this master craftsman at work. It is also no wonder that Henry became increasingly fond of this ray of sunshine that had entered his life. The energy from her vibrant personality reignited in him a spark that had been dormant for many years. She was real, vibrant, and brilliant, and she understood his work. Others in the community looked with curious wonder, as one would an aberration, a departure from the normal, but Loila understood.

She became a successful artist herself. She worked in oils and water colors, and her works were displayed widely.

Her brother, Ora, was studying dentistry at the University of Chicago. He wrote and informed her that a receptionist job could be hers if she would like to come to Chicago. She could stay with him and attend the art institute. She jumped at the opportunity and boarded a train for Chicago, leaving behind a very broken-up boyfriend, Albert Horner, an employee at Cardston Motors. They never did reunite. He left Cardston and settled in Coutts, Alberta. There, he operated a gas station and later became mayor.

Loila roomed with Ora in a seedy area of Chicago, hardly more than an arm's reach from the elevated. Every time a train sped past their flat, tremors rippled throughout the building, creating a deafening din. Chicago was in the throes of prohibition and crime ran out of control. Stills and speakeasies permeated the neighbourhood, and gangsters plied their trade with impunity.

Loila took the receptionist job at the dental school. Before long, several of the dental students became interested in her. She enjoyed the attention of having handsome young dental students hover over her, telling jokes and showing off. She became particularly attracted to one—a tall cowboy type from Texas with a keen and cultured mind.

"He already had a girl whom he was engaged to marry who was beautiful and dumb and I being just dumb didn't have a chance," complained Loila in her *Journal.*

But there were others. An unlikely candidate was Charles Ahner, an unsophisticated dental student in his junior year.

"He was spending entirely too much time at the information desk," complained Loila, "and finally asked me for a date. At first I thought I could never like [him] on account of his ugly shaped mouth."

She started going out with him, mainly on the recommendation of Ora, who was responsible for looking after her interests while she remained with him in "Hog Town." He saw Charles as an innocuous sort of chap; safe and reliable.

Charles, who came from a well-to-do Chicago family, took her to the best places to dine, and they danced to the music of the big bands. He introduced her to his family, and, while his parents seemed to be fond of Loila, they didn't know much about the Mormon religion, and they were skeptical about it.

Loila wrote in her *journal:*

> About the next Sunday we [Loila and Ora] asked Charles to go to church with us and he discovered the fact that the Church of Jesus Christ and the Mormon Church were synonymous. He seemed to like the church, however and was not prejudiced.... I shall never forget how surprised his mother was when I told her that it was against my religion to drink coffee and how she fussed about getting me something else.
>
> Charles thought nothing of spending $5.00 to take a girl out one evening as his father always shelled him out that much whenever he wanted it. Accordingly he took me many places which otherwise I could never [have] attended. We took in all the large show houses in Chicago and the best dance halls such as the Treenon, advertised as the world's most beautiful ball room at that time. We went to the DeMolay Round Up at one of the big hotels, several good sorority parties and fraternity parties.
>
> I shall never forget my 22nd birthday as we, that is Charles, Doc [Ora] and his girl friend and myself went to dinner at the Sherman Hotel, the world's largest. It was a five course dinner and when I didn't know what to do I waited for Charles and watched him. The first thing I or-

> dered was a blue point cocktail without having any idea of what it was made. They brought in a large silver plate containing five smaller divisions underlayed with ice. In the centre was a small dish of red sauce, and all around it were laid the biggest raw oysters I had ever seen. All I had to dissect them with was a small fork and when I tried to cut them into smaller pieces the slimy things jiggled and slid around and wouldn't be divided. When I looked up and saw my friend watching me with great amusement, I gave up the struggle. When I watched him stabbing the monsters and eating them whole after sousing them a bit in the catsup, I too sneaked up on one and stabbed him and swallowed him whole. I was goaded on by the appearance of the dough-faced waiter watching me, and so by hook or crook, I got rid of the oysters. The rest of the meal was very delightful.

It was rumored that she fell in love with Charles. Loila wanted much the same things most young ladies her age wanted in the 1920s: a devoted husband, a simple home, kids. It was a reasonable expectation, and one the Mormon Church encouraged. Loila wanted no less.

When she was about seventeen, a member of the church made the prediction that in due course Loila would enjoy the blessings of matrimony, motherhood and the benefits of a happy and comfortable home. This was encouraging to her, and she looked forward to a time when she would enjoy such a blessing. She planned for it. In her *Journal* she listed the duties of a wife and how to maintain a good marital relationship.

Upon completion of her art course, Loila returned to Cardston. A short time later Charles appeared on her doorstep, according to rumor. He wanted to marry her, but that didn't happen. Whether one or both of her parents objected, or whether the lovers decided to break it off, isn't known. It remains a family secret. He returned to Chicago and they never saw each other again. Loila remained single for the rest of her short life. The prediction she received of marital bliss never came true. Some believe she remained constant to the one and only love she ever had.

Loila turned her attention to her other interests—nature (especially wild flowers), art, and her Mormon faith. She enjoyed pack horse trips into the mountains, where she could bask in the loveliness of nature.

Henry was twenty-five years older than Loila. He had spent his entire young life living an illusion. He was a twentieth century throwback, practicing the medieval knightly behavior of unrequited love. He was an anachronism, living in an alien world. Now in his late forties, he was again toying with another bout of unrequited love with its attending pain—a pain he would rather endure than be free of, if it meant forgetting Loila.

Henry unloaded some of his most private thoughts on Charley. They were, however, always disguised by a subterfuge that Henry had mastered over the years.

He began talking to Charley about Loila all the time. When he'd be fashioning something for his house, he would ask: "Do you think she would like this?"

He told Charley how she resembled his girl in Belgium. He couldn't entirely let go of that image. He had lived with it too long, but it was fading. He could still bring to mind certain behavioral patterns, certain expressions, but they were becoming blurred. Now when he brought her image to mind, he found it difficult to hold on to it. The harder he tried, the more illusive it became, until her intangible form would evaporate in a mist, and Loila's image would emerge.

"Do you think she would like me," Henry would ask.

Charley tried to encourage him to ask her for a date. But Henry couldn't. He preferred unrequited love. It was safer. It protected him from the rejection he feared. Besides, he didn't believe he was good enough for her.

"She won't go with me." Henry argued. "She's Mormon. She wouldn't have me. She comes from a good family."

Loila continued her visits to the Rock House, never dreaming that Henry was growing more and more attached to her. What Henry didn't know was that Loila had also experienced the separation from a loved one she held dear and to whom she would remain true.

There was no solution for Loila, but there was for Henry. Some people in the community believed that Henry gradually transferred the devotion he held for the lady in Belgium to Loila, and the house became the instrument through which he would win her heart. His illusions could breech that obstacle. After a point, everything he did, he did for Loila.

8. Mentally Incompetant

HENRY'S mind began to deteriorate at an accelerated pace while working at Waterton. He became forgetful. Dreams began to take on a greater reality than reality itself. Sometimes he would become confused, but the quality of his work didn't diminish. His skill had become so automatic, that his hands appeared to live a separate life of their own. Like an automaton he worked, but his mind traveled elsewhere. The faded image of the girl in Belgium still haunted him, but it was receding like the galaxies in an expanding universe. He wanted it back. He needed that image. It was all he had, and he begged like a felon on the gallows.

He was becoming stranger even to himself. Sometimes he would talk to himself for a long while, taking no notice of those around him. He talked to the one phantom of the past he did not want to let go. His poor English would trail off into his native tongue and then back into English.

"You'd like it if you saw it. You'd change your mind," he would mumble to himself repeatedly, while his hands carried out the work as if they were guided by some unseen force. Then the fog would lift and his reason would return, which may have been more frightening to him than his delusions, because he must have known for a long time about the sickness that would eventually and certainly take away his reason and, perhaps, plunge him into a nightmare world of twisted forms and cacophonous sounds—a swirling world of no direction, no destination, and no escape.

Charley saw Henry deteriorating before his eyes. So did Robert. Both worried, but hoped that it was no more than a passing condition caused by overwork and stress.

Others saw it too, and rumors began to circulate.

"His girl sent him a 'Dear John' letter and he is heading for a nervous breakdown."

"His sweetheart was on her way to join him and was killed in a freak train accident."

His general behavior changed. He always removed his cap and coat when he came to breakfast at Nixon's Cafe in Waterton. As the sickness relentlessly invaded his brain, he started to forget such courtesies and had to be reminded. Henry would immediately comply humbly. "I'm sorry, I forgot."

Henry became increasingly cranky and reclusive. He didn't want anyone around him. He became erratic, emotional, and sometimes verbally abusive.

One morning, while Charley, Robert and Henry were getting ready to go to breakfast; Henry became extremely agitated. He mumbled incoherently and waved his hands nervously. He had lost his cap. They left the cabin and walked over to Nixon's cafe where they and many of the other workers took their meals. A large table was set for them and the meals were served family style. Henry was becoming loud. He kept complaining that he couldn't find his cap and that he must find it and that he didn't know where he had left it and that somebody might have taken it and he might never get it back. He looked all over but he couldn't find it.

The astonished men at the table sat silently and solemnly glanced knowingly at one another. The waitress entered the dining room and placed a large platter of pancakes in the middle of the table. Henry grabbed it and set it in front of himself. The waitress smiled warily and said, "Henry, those are for all the men."

"No," insisted Henry, "they are mine."

He began to pour syrup all over the pancakes. Again the men exchanged glances, and the waitress looked in bewilderment.

"I'll get another platter," she said, as she hurried back to the kitchen. Henry continued to grumble over his lost cap. He never touched the pancakes. He never took one bite.

"Lets go back to the cabin and help Henry find his cap," said Robert to Charley.

The three men got up from the table. The other men avoided Henry's eyes, as though his condition was contagious, but they looked at Charley and Robert and shook their heads sympathetically. Henry remained wound tight. He sputtered and fumed as they entered the cabin. They turned the place upside down, but didn't find the cap. Henry paced the floor like a caged wolf, and then began insisting that he had to return to Cardston.

"My wife is having a baby and she's in the hospital!" he shouted.

He pleaded to be taken back to Cardston.

Both men were shaken. Neither had ever experienced anything like this before. Robert told Charley to drive Henry back to Cardston and make sure he sees a doctor.

Henry seemed to recover his senses on the ride back to Cardston, and wanted to be let out at his house, but Charley insisted on taking Henry to see the local doctor. The doctor looked him over and then released him, probably with the admonition that he take better care of himself and get some rest. Charley reluctantly dropped Henry off at his house and returned to Waterton. He would look in on him on the weekend.

The house—a palace in a remote, treeless prairie, a cloistered kingdom in an alien culture—loomed before him. Here was his manor, the product of his skilled hands and dreams; an edifice built to honor and sequester her.

Henry began to work as soon as he got into the house. It was the only thing he could do anymore. Work is what he always did. Now, he didn't have to think anymore. Inertia had taken over. He worked automatically. Recently he experienced flashes or short periods of insanity. Now he experienced short flashes of sanity, emerging from chaos and confusion. During those short flashes a grim truth bore through the erosion of his diseased brain. At last, he knew that everything he did for her didn't matter any more. All that mattered was the creation itself. To create was to catch a glimpse of God. His reach had exceeded his grasp, but heaven still eluded him.

The veil dropped again, and in his vision a phantasmagoria of hexagonal shapes emitted from a point of singularity, rushed toward him, enormously increasing in size, only to again recede to its original point. Faces rushed toward him with hollow voices, reverberating in his soul. His weary mind cleared and came into focus again.

In the golden oak room, he sat in his rocker in front of his fireplace. Everything was serene. In quiet meditation his mind stalled on one thought. He was forty-eight-years-old and still not married. He must get married! He must have a wife with whom to share his house! He went out and wandered about the town. He proposed to every woman he met. Age made no difference. He asked young and old, married and single, those he knew and those he didn't. He knocked on doors and went from house to house looking for a bride, offering his house into the bargain.

A stunned community shook their heads in disbelief. They grieved over this gifted recluse who came to live among them and created so much beauty and they prayed for him.

He returned home, his quest unfulfilled. His life unfulfilled. While members of the community gathered to decide what to do about Henry, he sat brooding in front of the fireplace. He became aware of something moving outside his window. A cow had wandered into his yard and was peacefully grazing on tufts of grass. To Henry, this was an intruder—a trespasser on his property! He did not want trespassers on his property! The fury of a demon possessed him! He ran out of the house screaming invectives! Grabbing a garden hoe, he viciously attacked the unoffending animal. He chased after it and furiously beat on it until he had chopped a hole out of the poor beast's hide.

Fearful onlookers summoned the police, who took Henry into custody. By then he was exhausted. He became cogent long enough to declare that he could no longer take care of himself. He asked to be hospitalized. The police transported him to Alberta Hospital at Ponoka, the Provincial hospital for the mentally insane, on June 2, 1928. His estimated age was forty-eight. He arrived in an incoherent state, and he spoke very little. He gave hospital staff no information concerning next of kin or place and date birth. Police later discovered from a friend of Henry's that he had a sister living in Brussels, Belgium at 300 Block, Avenue de la St. Louis. Her name wasn't known and a search revealed no such address in Brussels. Authorities never found a next of kin.

At the time of his admission, Ponoka's Medical Superintendent found Henry to be mentally incompetent. He officially diagnosed him as suffering from a condition known as General Paralysis of the Insane. There being no known next of kin, the diagnosis resulted in placing Henry's estate under the control of the Administrator of Estates for the Mentally Incompetent. The following document officially placed Henry's estate at the discretion of the province under the responsibility of the Justice Department:

File: 4373L

IN THE MATTER OF THE ESTATES OF THE MENTALLY INCOMPETENT ACT

-and-

IN THE MATTER OF THE ESTATE OF Henry Hoet (A Mental Incompetent)

I HEREBY CERTIFY that Henry Hoet

of Cardston in the Province of Alberta,

is a mentally incompetent person and

is now detained in the Provincial Mental Hospital at

Ponoka, pursuant to the provisions of The Mental Diseases Act.

AND I FURTHER CERTIFY that TRENHOLME DICKSON under the

provisions of The Estates of the Mentally Incompetent Act is

the Administrator of the Estate of the said Henry Hoet.

Dated at Edmonton, Alberta, this 21 st day of June A.D. 1928.

Deputy Attorney General

When Charley and his dad came home for the weekend, they learned that Henry had been taken away. They never saw him again.

Not long after his incarceration, a rumor of his death circulated and was widely believed for many years.

In 1981 a paper entitled "Cobblestone Manor" prepared for Alberta Culture, Historical Resources, Historic Site Service, the author R.M. Massey, wrote "...he [Henry Hoet] was committed to a mental institution in Ponoka, where he died soon after." In fact, he didn't die in Ponoka, and he didn't die soon after being committed there. He lived another twenty years.

Henry Hoet vanished within Ponoka's walls. All contact with the outside world ceased. All of his creative energy ceased. He would never build again. All that he did create was taken away. The tools he so delicately fashioned to fit his hands fell into lesser skilled hands, and there was no one to know or care. For whatever reason, he had given up family years earlier. He made no close friends. He was alone with no one to protect his interests, no one to encourage him, no one to extend a warm sympathetic smile, and no one who knew and could acknowledge the extent of his creative genius. Those in Cardston who might have cared, genuinely believed him to be dead.

Ponoka kept Henry's hospital records for the required period after his death in 1949, and then shredded them, erasing from posterity another tragic segment of his life.

9. Abandoned

THE Rock House stands abandoned now, its interior dark and still. The rhythmic beat of the hammer and the resonant scrape of the chisel are silent. There is no crackling fire in the fireplace, casting shadows on the wall. A cold draft wafts down the chimney and stirs the left-over ash. The symphony is over. There is no applause. The maestro is gone. Silence reigns, but for the eerie cry of the wind, winging about the stone walls.

Veteran Constable Jack Reid of "D" Division of the Alberta Provincial Police surveys the abandoned house. He is an iron-willed lawman in his late forties. He is not given to maudlin sentimentality. Yet, something does not feel good within him, as he wanders through the Rock House amid all the unique furnishings and exquisite artisanship. Amid all the splendor, there is an oppressive emptiness, a futility engraved in rock.

Listing every item in every room, Constable Reid moves Methodically through the house. He marvels at the bazaar beauty, but, to him, it seems the most gloomy place to call a house one can imagine. The painstaking contortions of small bits of hardwood inlay and stained glass, forming thousands of geometric shapes in chaotic confusion and order at the same time, seems to express a mental derangement Reid thought. "All too apparent in its designer." But there is simultaneously an overwhelming aura of genius present, like a hovering specter, throughout the edifice.

He knew Henry and was always fond of him, although he always thought that he was as crazy as a bed bug. He admired him for his incredible skill; respected him for his quiet dignity. He will miss his eccentric acquaintance.

Reid notes that the house is wired from the town system but has its own water system, consisting of a big pressure tank with a hand pump. The roof leaks in one spot, and, in the basement, Reid finds a foot of water, the result of a recent flood. He makes one last cursory examination of each room and locks the house. He arranges with a local resident to board up some of the windows and pump the water out of the basement. Then he returns to his office and writes his report to J. O. Scott, Sub-Inspector Commanding "D" Division. In it he says:

> I have taken some time to make this investigation as the case is an unfortunate one.
>
> This man is a Belgian by birth and the finest carpenter and cabinet maker ever known in this district. He has lived here for years without relatives or close friends. [He] acquired an old log dwelling in south Cardston and built into and onto it for fourteen years. [He] put the finest hard wood—oak and maple—and the most exquisite workmanship into its finish, fixtures and furniture, making every piece of furniture and fixtures, paneling, etc. by hand.
>
> He told me that he had put some $10,000 to $15,000 worth of materials into the place.
>
> No one has ever lived in it but Hoet. It is still unfinished....

Fearing a break in or damage by the elements (there was no insurance on the contents of the house), Reid strongly suggests that arrangements be made to:

> rent the place, or even allow a responsible party to live in it to take care of it until it can finally be disposed of.... No one would buy it at anything like its value for a home, though it is suggested it might make a desirable country club house. However, it would seem unlikely that such a club would be organized here. It could be dismantled and the valuable wood work removed in panels, fixtures and furniture likewise, and sold if a market could be found.

Reid also reports that the property is mortgaged. Dr. Harry B. Stackpool, Cardston's obstetrician, anesthetist, druggist and businessman, holds a three hundred dollar mortgage on the house. Another three hundred dollar mortgage was placed on the property on June 2, 1928, for notes given at various times, during the fall of 1927, for furniture, which included two upholstered davenports, six rocking chairs, two dining room sideboards, and two leather upholstered chairs.

These purchases seem extravagant for a man who made almost everything with his own hands. But, one of the symptoms of his mental condition is delusions of grandeur. Design, structure, building materials, furniture, and interior fittings, incorporated into the Rock House, bear witness to symptoms confirming that Henry must have suffered such delusions for a long time. Shortly before being hospitalized, his grand delusions greatly increased.

Henry's estate faced the possibility of a law suit from a supplier of building materials. He is alleged to have ordered $123.08 worth of materials that were never accepted on arrival and were left in the hands of the railroad company.

Constable Reid reports that he had been unable to find any valuable papers or documents. Letters, especially from Belgium, would have been important. It would have given the police a lead that might have revealed the existence of relatives. But, there were no letters.

Sub-Inspector J. O. Scot received the report and forwarded it to the Commissioner with the following comments:

> I personally visited this man some years ago, and would advise that, should this man be detained for any length of time in the Mental Hospital, that the Department take the necessary steps to protect the goods in question, as it will be noted that this man, who is an expert cabinet maker, apparently has been spending most of his time in the manufacture of book cases, reading lamps, piano lamps, etc., many of which took months of expert workmen's labour, and are of considerable value..., being composed of hundreds of pieces of inlaid oak.

Both Constable Reid and Scott took more than a passing interest in Henry's estate. Reid frequently checked the property and continued to insist in his reports that, "someone be put in the place, without rent if necessary, to keep it from becoming run down. There is too much value on the inside of the place."

Reid made sure the house was periodically aired out and the yard mowed, and he never stopped pressuring the authorities to get someone in the house to take care of it and to protect its contents.

In his November 11th report, he informed headquarters that some boys had pried open a door and got in. Fortunately, nothing was disturbed or taken. Reid refastened the door, but he remained fearful that, if steps were not taken to get someone to take care of the place, things would start to go missing and serious damage might be done by vandals. Again he pleaded:

> ... as I have pointed out in previous reports there is valuable property there which might be either stolen or damaged. The suggestion of damage by mice is well founded. Leaking roofs is another source of damage. I certainly don't guarantee that it wont be broken into and articles stolen or damaged. I have suggested that someone be put in it to live, rent free, if necessary to prevent loss. That suggestion is repeated. I can give it no further care than has been done. And it has been about five months since this man left here for Ponoka.

Finally, in December, someone was found (supposedly a friend of Henry's) to take care of the property. The person agreed to keep the place clean and free of mice. The leaking roof was repaired, being nothing more than a few metal shingles, dislodged during a recent storm.

The house was now adequately secured, but, to dispense with it, was another question. Constable Reid discussed the matter with several of Cardston's responsible people, but no one could come up with a reasonable plan. They all knew that the contents of the house were of the highest quality and should bring a good price, but, it was doubtful that such items could be sold in Cardston and the surrounding area, especially now, during hard economic times. The two big chesterfield suits were suitable only for a club room or a hotel lobby. Few homes could use the other big items. Reid believed that a buyer might be found for the Oak paneling, which could be carefully removed from the walls and ceiling. The house could then be finished in a more conventional style, which might improve the chances of selling it.

A decision had to be made and soon. There was the matter of the two mortgages on the house. Interest charges had swelled the money owed to Dr. Stackpool to $361.21 and $320.70 to a local bank. Both holders were willing to agree to any suggestion that would respect their claim, and, at the same time, save for the estate all that could be realized out of it. But, as long as these obligations were unpaid, the interest would continue to make ever greater claims on the estate.

Reid again expressed his serious misgivings about the province being able to obtain the real value of the estate. Location was its biggest drawback. Cardston was a farming community. There wasn't a market for such a building, even in good economic times. The basement occasionally flooded during heavy rains or when the spring run-off overflowed Lee's Creek. The house was located two blocks from the main street on a very poor road. The massiveness of the house precluded any possibility of it being moved to another location, where it might serve as a tourist attraction or some kind of club house.

Reid believed that the furnishings could be sold in Calgary or some other large centre. A local merchant was asked to estimate its value. His conclusion was not optimistic. Because of the uniqueness of the furniture, he believed that its real value could not be realized. This prompted Inspector Scott to request permission and authority to arrange for an auction sale of the Hoet estate. What couldn't be sold at auction would be transported to Calgary.

Permission was granted and Scott began negotiating with an auction house in Lethbridge. The auction house agreed to accept a five per cent commission plus mileage and expenses, providing all articles be included in the sale. It agreed to distribute handbills to residents within a twenty-five mile radius of Cardston as well as to Waterton National Park with the hope of attracting curious tourists. The sale would take place after the harvesting of crops in the area to insure a larger attendance. The auctioneer also promised to notify parties he knew were interested in furniture.

10. The Auction

BY order of the Government of Alberta, Henry Hoet's house and other belongings were scheduled to go on sale October 5, 1929. The auction was widely advertised. Circulars were mailed throughout the area and notices posted in neighbouring towns and villages. Ads appeared in the *Lethbridge Herald* and the *Cardston News*. It was billed as:

AUCTION SALE

EXTRAORDINARY

of the Henry Hoet Estate, Cardston

ON OCTOBER 5, 1929, AT 1 p.m. SHARP

Under instructions received by Administrator Mr. Trenholme Dickson we will offer by Public Auction the Estate of Henry Hoet, situated two blocks from the Main Street of Cardston on the south side of Lees Creek. These goods are the work of a genius which has taken 14 years to make and all by hand. Anyone seeking real genuine, massive, and unusual in appearance Furniture, will be well advised not to miss this sale, as we do not know of anything in Alberta to compare. Reme[m]ber all hand made and different, some wonderful pieces for club rooms and hotels, as well as homes.

Hereunder is a partial list:

Southwest room with removable interior fittings.

22 Oak Panels 26 in. x 6 ft. edged with 3 1/2 x 11 1/2 Oak Strips.

6 Oak Panels 10 to 19 inches x 6 ft., to match.

137 Oak Panels 26 inches x 26 inches, ornamented to match.

11 light Chandelier Ceiling Panels, 26 x 26 to match stained glass and ornamental figured.

8 door panels

2 large Oak Doors with stained glass and ornamental figured.

Large stone Fireplace with Oak and Stained Glass Bookcases and cupboards for 6 ft. on each side.

Southeast Room

10 Oak Panels 24 in. x 5 ft. 3 in., edged with 3 1/2 x 1 1/2 in. solid Oak Stripes.

10 Oak Panels 12 to 18 in. x 5 ft. 3 in., to match.

30 Oak Panels 16 x 23 in. top and bottom of walled figured.

126 plus many fitted parts of panels, hexagon shaped, 24 x 24 figured.

2 ornamental Oak Paneled Doors.

One Green Mohair Upholstered Chesterfield. Very massive.

Three Large Rockers to match.

One Large Blue Mohair Chesterfield.

Three Large Arm Chairs to match.

One Large Chintz covered Rocker.

13 Medium sized Leather and Chintz covered Rockers, some Oak and some Fir, all solid.

13 Oak and Fir Leather Seated Dining Chairs.

One White Enameled Kitchenette.

One Solid Fir Kitchenette.

One White Enameled K. Table with Drawer.

Two Solid Fir Library Tables with two drawers each

One Solid Fir Buffet with Mirror.

Two Solid Oak Buffet with Mirror and ornamental stained glass doors.

Three Solid Oak China Cabinets.

One Brussels Rug, 10 x 14.

Two Wardrobes 7 ft. high.

One 4 ft. 6 in. Walnut Bed, complete.

Two new Slumber King Springs 4.6.

Two Sp. filled Mattresses 4.6.

24 pieces Oak Veneer 4 x 1 1/2 ft.

Three pieces Walnut Veneer 4 x 1 1/2 ft.

Hundreds of Oak Scraps.

One 2-hole Burner Oil Stove.

One Cabinet Maker's bench.

Two Wood Vises, Maples.

One 10 x 12 ft. Tent and fly, 12 oz. each.

A lot of dandy Cabinet Maker's tools, the best money can buy.

Two Medicine Cabinets.

Pots and Pans, Glassware, Pictures, 55 piece China Set.

New Plumbing Fixtures, such as Bath Tub, Basin, Toilet, and numerous and valuable articles, that are not mentioned.

THE HOUSE AND LAND WILL ALSO BE SOLD
TERMS: STRICTLY CASH
BONFADINI'S LTD.
LETHBRIDGE RELIABLE AUCTIONEERS...

On the day of the auction, the auctioneer and his two assistants left Lethbridge at seven in the morning and arrived in Cardston about an hour later.

Hundreds of people from Hillspring, Leavitt, Aetna, Kimball, and other neighbouring communities flocked to the auction. Everyone knew about the Rock House and its eccentric builder. Everyone wanted a piece of it. It started at one o'clock in the afternoon. Ten pictures sold, some for as low as one dollar. The highest price paid for a picture was four dollars. Those who knew Henry wanted a memento with which to remember him. Kettles and jugs, pots and pans went under the gavel, bringing anywhere from fifty cents to one dollar and seventy-five cents.

One young girl, Zina Jacobs, desperately wanted something of Henry's, but times were tough, and her family had no money to give her. She cried all day and complained bitterly, "If I only had five dollars, I could buy one of Henry's tables."

Six dining chairs sold for twenty-two dollars. A mirror went for three dollars and twenty-five cents, and a library table for sixteen dollars. Two rockers sold for eleven dollars a piece.

Zina never got the memento she wanted to remind her of the magical moments she watched Henry cast his spell over the raw materials he could deftly convert into beautiful objects.

An old wood plain sold for fifty cents. Two better ones for three dollars a piece. A saw and a plain together sold for one-fifty.

The people kept coming. More tools went: saws, clamps, hacksaws, files, and the miter box Henry used to delicately cut the hardwood scraps that fit perfectly into his panels. Women marveled over Henry's taste in house furnishings. They bid on curtains and blinds. Seven more dining chairs sold; all brought twenty-seven dollars. Four more rockers sold at thirteen dollars a piece. A carpet brought sixteen dollars. More rockers. Henry's beautiful stained glass that he had not cut—the glass he waited for so impatiently—brought a dollar. Another library table—seventeen dollars. Henry's treasured Little Big books—a dollar. Reading these books was one of Henry's few pleasures.

The day drew on. The auctioneer barked rapid fire, proceeding as fast as he could. Still there seemed to be no end of items. A tent, a dinner set, vases, paneling.

The prairie sun, like a golden coin, edged westward and the auctioneer continued to shout incomprehensible phrases and point out at the crowd accusingly. A Dinner set, tea set, lamps, a china cabinet, buffets, sofas—things to entice his fiancee to join him. Boxes of tools, brooder houses, fishing gear, stoves. Years of dreams vanished with the wave of a hand, the nod of a head. The sun sank behind the horizon. A rosy glow washed the prairies, and still the auctioneer performed his gyrations into the velvet night under electric lights. The real prize was yet to come.

Midnight. All was gone. The house like a ravaged maiden stood empty, unprotected by its ravaged master. And the naked walls reverberated Wordsworth's plaintive refrain:

"Whither is fled the visionary gleam?
Where is it now, the glory and the dream?"

The house at last went on the block. A reasonable estimate of its actual value with all its fittings and decorations was placed at twenty to twenty-five thousand dollars.

The crowd had dwindled to a few.

"Sold for one thousand five hundred dollars!" shouted the exhausted auctioneer, pointing to Canon S. H. Middleton, the Masonic Lodge Chief Official who had been authorized by the Masons to bid on the house. They thought it would make an excellent meeting lodge.

After expenses, the sale grossed $2,560. Nearly four hundred dollars would go to Dr. Stackpool. Other of Henry's obligations would also have to be paid. The remainder would go to the provincial government to help cover the cost of caring for Henry, who, on the night of the sale, lie down in a ward with fifty-nine other men. His neighbour on the left lay three feet away; the one on the right, three feet away. There were no stained glass lamps, no panels, no tools, no fireplaces, no books, no hope.

The house sold at a fraction of its true value, leaving Henry in a state of penury, completely dependent for all his needs on the generosity of the provincial government.

Trenholme Dickson, Administrator of Estates of the Mentally Incompetent, admitted in his Affidavit of Transfer: "In my representative capacity I am without sufficient information to enable me to complete clauses 2, 3, and 5, to this Affidavit." Number 2 of this Affidavit states "The improvements upon the said land at the date I purchased the same were of the fair value of $----------."

Dickson left the line blank.

He did not think it necessary to bring in an outside expert to estimate the true value of the house. Instead, he, on behalf of the government, retained a local lawyer to make that evaluation. In a sworn statement on the Affidavit of Transferee, he estimated the true value of the house and lot to be one thousand five hundred dollars.

The Masons took possession of the Rock House and hired a Belgian couple as live-in caretakers. The Bergmans with their young son and daughter took up residence.

The house was sold in 1929, the year the Great Depression began. Cardston had felt its sting long before it was officially recognized. Harold Salway had left Cardston before Henry Hoet had been institutionalized. There was nothing much for him in Cardston, so he determined to seek his fortune elsewhere. He lived the life of a hobo, riding the rails here and there, doing odd jobs when they could be found, but he learned, as millions of others had, that fortunes aren't readily made in a depression, and so he returned home.

He began dating a local girl by the name of Unice Sherwood. After a short courtship, he asked her to be his wife. The marriage took place in 1936 on the lawn of the bride's parents' home, a little more than a kilometre from the Rock House. The newly-weds learned that a shivery had been planned. To thwart the would-be kidnappers, they escaped during a lull in the celebration. Hand in hand Harold and his bride, trailing her wedding gown, took off on a dead run, clambered down the creek bank and into the water, and scrambled up the creek to the Rock House. Mr. Bergman was surprised to see the pair rush into his home without knocking. The fugitives explained as best they could to Bergman, who spoke very little English, what was happening. The Bergmans were made to understand that the newly-weds needed their protection.

Bergman, a big, burley man, picked up a stick the size of a baseball bat and positioned himself at the door, while Harold and his bride spent their wedding night sleeping in the glassed-in verandah of the house, built by Henry for him and his would-be bride.

That night, Henry, under the protection of men dressed in white, climbed into his bed amid the shuffling sounds of the others who shared his ward, and, though surrounded by a throng of people within arm's reach, he would forever be alone. He had given himself to love and loyalty, and now there was no self left. He curled into a fetal position and sought oblivion in merciful sleep.

His house, in the meantime, protected and sheltered the nuptials on their honeymoon night. At least, the house fulfilled the purpose for which it was built.

The Masons would maintain ownership of the Rock House for the next thirty years, finally selling it in a dilapidated state in 1959.

For a time, caretakers lived in the house and maintained it. The Masons used it for meetings and special occasions. But, the depression, like a maelstrom, sucked wealth and spirit from the people into a vortex, leaving neither money to maintain the Rock House nor interest in it. It was boarded up and abandoned, like its builder, to the ravages of time and decay.

Tales, that the house was haunted by Henry Hoet's ghost, began to circulate. For many years, no one could be found to buy or rent it. Only the neighbourhood children, with their unquenchable thirst for adventure, risked an encounter with Henry's spirit and entered the mysterious sanctum. The Lee's Creek swimming hole was still a main attraction for kids in the area, and they no longer had to worry about being chased off by Henry and his dog. The children also believed the house was haunted. That led to many dares, and few red-blooded Canadian urchins can resist a dare. So, on occasions, some of the brave avant guard would sneak gingerly into the dark and musty confines of the oaken rooms, adorned with the panels from which draped intricately formed spider webs. When none of the invaders were consumed by the diaphanous ectoplasm of Henry's ghost, an army of lesser heroes and heroines followed. In their innocent play, they vandalized the house. Many made off with interesting souvenirs. They especially liked to find pieces of the Italian stained glass that they used as hop scotch markers.

If the house had indeed been haunted, it would have had to be haunted by someone other than Henry. Henry was alive and would live on for many more years. But they would not be producing years. His once creative mind was addled, his skilled hands idle. They swung back and forth in continuous meaningless motion, as he shuffled aimlessly in his misty world of illusions.

11. Oliver

In October 16, 1932, Henry Hoet was transferred from Alberta Hospital Ponoka to Alberta Hospital Edmonton (Oliver). He arrived in a van with several other transferees. He was processed and assigned to a ward he would share with about sixty other men. The hospital population was approximately three hundred fifty. All men. Years later women were admitted, but they were strictly segregated from male patients and male nurses.

About seventy percent of the patients came from rural Alberta. They were victims of a lonely, harsh, insecure life. The land off which they tried to survive was boss, niggardly, and mean. It sucked the spirit out of its tenants, and spit them out, when they were spent. It teased a little here and a little there. It promised prosperity with just a little more work, a little more luck, a little more sacrifice. When success was within reach, the elements would conspire to tear from their callous hands the fruit of their labour—a devastating hail, a drought, an early snow. There were long isolated winters with icy winds and drifting snow; the eerie howl of wind and coyote; cabin fever, and those voices in the night.

Approximately eighty percent were economically dependent, or in fear of being in want. They were the losers in life's great competition, and the depression of the "dirty thirties" didn't help. For these ravaged souls, Alberta Hospital Edmonton (Oliver) seemed a haven in an otherwise frightening and uncomfortable world.

But that was not Henry's problem. He was an artist and an artisan who had been highly paid for his skill. He had built and owned a home like no other in southern Alberta. His problem was not environmental. It was biological. Henry's mental illness was inevitable. His condition was predictable, and he probably knew for years what his ultimate fate would be. Perhaps that's why he left Belgium, his family and loved ones. Maybe that's why he never mentioned names or the city from which he came. Henry contracted a disease, easily treated today, but not then. He suffered from general paralysis of the insane—syphilis. Everyone acquainted with Henry, knew about his "bride to be," but it is probable that Henry knew that the only love he would ever experience would be unrequited love. It is possible that his "bride to be" was merely a fantasy concocted by himself to provide him with a reason to strive. Robertson Davies, in his book *World of Wonders*, said, "Love does not demand to be requited, and can be a force where it is obviously hopeless." Did that force become Henry's creative genius?

Syphilis was the diagnosis, but, Dr. Alan Gordon, Vice President of Clinical Services at Alberta Hospital Edmonton, pointed out, in a telephone interview in 1994, that diagnosis in 1928 was not as accurate as it is today. So, while there is strong evidence, pointing to his having syphilis, it is not absolutely certain. All of his symptoms, however, pointed in that direction.

Dr. Violet Myers, who practiced for many years at Alberta Hospital Edmonton, starting in 1950, confirmed on August 20, 1994, that General Paralysis of the Insane is another way of saying syphilis. She said that Henry would have been in a general ward and would have been treated with antibiotics, especially penicillin after 1942.

Richard M. Restak, M.D. in his book *The Brain* states:

> ...behavioral disturbances sometimes prove irrelevant to understanding and treating the underlying illness. For instance, the psychoses associated with deficiencies of vitamin B6, syphilis, and inflammations of the brain are indistinguishable on behavioral grounds alone. One patient looks and sounds much like another. The specific diagnosis is reached only by observing the patient's response to medication (an antibiotic to cure inflammations, or vitamin B6 for the specific deficiency), or his or her reaction to certain tests (a positive blood test for syphilis). In each instance biological measures provide keener insights into the nature of the illness than behavioral observations alone.

Henry could very well have suffered from a vitamin B6 deficiency, given the way he neglected the most rudimentary rules of good health, but certainly, as a patient in a modern hospital, enjoying a healthy diet, his psychotic symptoms would have disappeared; but they didn't.

The *Dictionary of Psychology* by James P. Chaplin defines paresis as, "a psychosis accompanied by progressive paralysis. Paresis is caused by syphilis of the nervous system. *Syns.* general paresis; Dementia Paralytica; paretic psychosis; general paralysis of the insane" and psychosis as "a severe mental disorder characterized by disorganization of the thought processes, disturbances in emotionality, disorientation as to time, space, and person, and, in some cases, hallucinations, and delusions."

Mental changes include gradual deterioration of personality, impaired concentration and judgment, loss of memory, and apathy or violent rages. Convulsions are not uncommon. Paranoia is a classical long-term symptom. It occurs most frequently in men between thirty-five and fifty years of age. Henry was about forty-eight.

At the behavioral level the psychosis assumes different patterns, at times resembling that of schizophrenia, at others that of cerebral arteriosclerosis. Most typical, however, is the expansive paretic, a grandiose, euphoric psychotic, who may claim to be a millionaire, a great inventor, or a genius. He lacks insight, his judgment is very poor, and his behavior is impulsive and capricious.

Since symptoms of involvement of the nervous system are usually delayed for about fifteen to twenty-five years after the initial infection, Henry could have been anywhere between twenty-three and thirty-three years of age when he contacted the infection. It is likely he contacted the disease in Belgium or New York as a young man.

It is not known when or where Henry contracted syphilis. It certainly wasn't a rare disease at the turn of the century. Douglas Neil Sprague in his book *Post Confederation Canada: The Structure of Canadian History Since Confederation* points to a much quoted study of New York City, which concluded: "...roughly one in five adults was infected with one or both diseases [syphilis and gonorrhea]; the two combined accounted for one quarter of all blindness and sterility, nearly three quarters of miscarriages, and half of something called 'terminal brain disease.'"

Henry not only suffered because of, at least, one act of sexual indiscretion, but also because of bad luck. He had a fifty-fifty chance of the disease being relatively benign. The flip of the coin came down on the side of life-long incapacitation. His condition progressed into Neurosyphilis and resembled other neurological disorders resulting in widespread destruction of brain tissue.

Being confined to Alberta Hospital (Oliver) could not have been pleasant for Henry. He had always been independent. Now he was restricted to hospital regimentation. He had always worked with his hands and mind. Now he was reduced to shuffling aimlessly about in slippers. He had enjoyed space and solitude. Now his space consisted of a bed in a large ward, not a breath away from his neighbours, in what was sometimes a chamber of chaos.

To make things worse, these were depression years. The hospital faced a critical shortage of money, supplies, and most importantly staff, who had to work twelve-hour shifts for very little pay. In the early thirties, nurses were paid around twenty-seven cents an hour. The hospital operated in somewhat of a holding pattern. A dedicated staff did what they could, but significant progress proved impossible.

From the time of Oliver's humble beginnings, its admissions increased annually. Oliver came to serve as an adjunct to Alberta Hospital (Ponoka) where all of Alberta's admissions were screened. Most of Oliver's patients were transfers from there, as was Henry. Most suffered chronic mental illnesses with little chance of recovery. Some of the staff complained that Oliver had become Ponoka's dumping ground. It began receiving increased numbers of the worst chronic patients from Ponoka. Many proved difficult to manage and all but impossible to treat. Some were extremely violent and dangerous and would attack members of the staff, biting, kicking, pinching. Some threw feces on the walls and smeared it on themselves and urinated on the floor. They could not be given forks or other sharp objects. They had to eat out of paper dishes.

Fortunately, these patients were kept separate from the more docile ones, among whom would have been Henry. In Cardston, people often described Henry as a quiet eccentric or a quiet genius. He demonstrated the same qualities at Oliver, minus the genius. Most of those who worked with him never knew of the creative talent he once had.

Given the mode of the times, when mental illness was considered a blight on a family—something almost evil, something to be hidden—it is not surprising that most of the patients were abandoned by their families and friends and left to languish alone behind the forbidden walls of mental institutions. People accepted familial and social isolation of mental patients as normal. Even some of the patients themselves did.

One of the doctors in residence, at the time Henry was at Oliver, told the following story about one of his patients:

> I am making the rounds and I see a bearded man standing looking out the window, a real Jewish patriarch, so I go up to him and say 'Shalom'. He nearly turned white. The attendant said he'd been there over 16 years. I noticed he wouldn't eat pork—a touch with reality—so I told the dietician he had an allergy and should have dairy products instead. One night he had a stroke and when I looked at his

> chart, it said "No next-of-kin". Years later I saw a notice in an Anglo-Jewish newspaper from New York, "Children seeking long-lost father", and it was him. The son was sure he knew what had happened. The old man's family was prominent—one son a doctor, another a lawyer, and so on—so when he had a mental breakdown in Canada, he decided to become a nonentity rather than stigmatize his family....

Is this what Henry did when he left his family years before? Did he leave for fear that he might disgrace his family if his illness became known? He must have known that he had syphilis. He must have known of what might be his ultimate fate. Karl Leszynski, a nurse employed in the ward in which Henry spent the last two years of his life, believes that to be the case.

Because of budgetary restraints, the staff at Oliver could provide nothing but the most basic physical needs. To maintain good hygiene, clearly established and closely followed routines governed sleeping, dressing, washing, and eating. Patients were encouraged to be physically active and take part in the maintenance of the ward. Such activities included scrubbing, window cleaning, floor polishing, and bed making.

Head nurse in the 1930s, Bill Raistrick, tells of Henry with his stumbling gate and head hanging down "wandering all over the place, pushing a polishing block along the floors."

By 1936 the patient population at Oliver had increased to around five hundred. Because of meager funding, there was nothing for patients to do but trivial chores and wandering aimlessly around the ward. In 1937 rooms for crafts opened, but its effect was limited, because of a shortage of staff.

The hospital tried to promote recreation, but it was of the most rudimentary form—simple organized events like kicking balls back and forth. Silent movies had been popular, but that died with funding restraints and no movies were shown for several years.

There are no records to tell us how Henry adjusted to his hospital environment, or in what activities he took part. The only employee, who remembers Henry from the thirties, was Bill Raistrick, and he doesn't remember much, because he was mainly attached to the dangerous inmates. He only caught glimpses of Henry now and then, pushing his polishing block. Raistrick believes that Henry's condition had already in the early 1930s progressed to the point where he could do little else. It is possible that he performed other menial tasks. It is also likely that he remained reclusive. Most of the people still living, that worked at the hospital while Henry was there, do not remember him. During the twenty years he was a patient, he made little impression on those around him. When he talked about his accomplishments, no one believed him. People suffering from general paralysis of the insane tend to display delusions of grandeur. Who would have believed that this destitute wreck had built a fabulous mansion or did the finishing work in the Mormon Temple and the Prince of Wales Hotel? The former staff members I interviewed were totally surprised to learn that he accomplished the things he did.

The patients and staff did constitute a community, of which Henry was a part. It was a community where eccentricity was the norm. It featured dead dreams and little hope. But however aberrant a mind becomes, there always remains, however dim, a driving spirit that sporadically ignites and revives a modicum of life and a trace of hope, from which efforts can spring that can appear bazaar.

Take for instance a shack town that arose on the remote fringes of the hospital grounds. Some of the patients found a burning pit on the hospital grounds from which they could take scraps—lumber, corrugated tin, cardboard, wire, and an assortment of other cast away materials. From this waste, little huts and shanties sprung up. They were decorated after each builder's fashion into something of theirs.

"They needed something to call their own, a little privacy, their own little home and their own little town," remarked one of the employees.

While money was tight and there were shortages, food was plentiful. The hospital became as self-sufficient as possible. A nine- hundred-acre farm, located on the grounds, supplied the patients and staff with meat, dairy products, eggs and vegetables. It also provided a place where patients could enjoy a few simple, healthy, outdoor tasks. Some patients cultivated their own garden plots.

The hospital furnished tobacco for those patients who enjoyed smoking. It was usually distributed after breakfast or lunch. Psychiatric nurse Reginald H. Smith recalls the daily ritual:

> Airmail tobacco was the main tobacco smoked. It stunk! The patients would line up in the middle of the ward floors and the ward Charge would say, "Tobacco boys!" and he'd have a great big pail of tobacco. They'd hold their left hand out and get a big pinch of tobacco and they'd hold their right hand out and get a half a dozen cigarette papers. Then they were moved to one side to get their smokes. It was the quietest time of the day.

Another of the daily events that lightened up the otherwise monotonous routine was the laundry delivery. Not that laundry in itself was of great interest, but the one delivering it was. He was George the horse. He had been a part of the institution for as long as most of the patients and staff could remember. He knew his route well. When he delivered a bundle of laundry to one station, George the horse would head unerringly to his next stop, but not until rewarded appropriately for his efforts. He would absolutely refuse to move on until given a carrot or a sugar cube.

Animals have a soothing affect on most people, especially on those who are lonely and abandoned. People love to love animals. Everyone at the hospital loved George, and he seemed to return that affection. Unfortunately, George suffered an accident that resulted in a broken leg. He had to be shot.

The end of the depression did not bring the expected improvement in conditions. The war intervened to sponge up funds and staff—especially staff. Many joined the military. Others moved into jobs that paid more money for shorter hours, resulting in a large turnover in hospital staff. Many of the newly hired hospital personnel could barely write their names. Qualifications for employment was reduced to grade eight. Even then, there were few takers for the low wages and long hours that were offered. So, the hospital limped on in its penurious state, the only increase being patients. During the war years the number of patients at Oliver rose to between nine hundred and a thousand.

Some of the increased population came with the opening of the first women's ward. They were an unruly group of transfers from Ponoka. They arrived in vans. Dressed in plain dresses, mackinaws and oversized galoshes, they spilled out of the vans and were ushered toward the building that would be their new home. Some wore restraining jackets. Male and female patients were strictly segregated, as were male and female nurses, who enjoyed little professional or personal contact.

An overworked and under trained staff stretched themselves to the limit, and none put in more time and effort than Dr. William Jonas McAlister. He had been appointed medical superintendent of the hospital on December 31, 1931. The ubiquitous doctor seemed to be at the hospital twenty-four hours a day. He lived on the grounds, and his one recreation was gardening.

He had the habit of slipping into the hospital any time of the day or night. When he was off duty, he wore an old torn brown sweater and an old pair of pants. He would shuffle around the hospital in soft slippers, making himself indistinguishable from the patients. On one occasion, a newly hired male nurse mistook him for a patient. When McAlister tried to explain who he was, the new employee replied "yah, they all say that."

The wards remained shorthanded throughout the war. The nursing service functioned at about fifty percent under strength. Lack of supervision in the dining hall led to increased fighting among patients. Overcrowded wards caused serious problems, especially in the chronic wards, one of which housed Henry. About ninety patients now filled each ward.

Staff followed routine strictly. Everything was done exactly on time. Any deviation could upset the patients. For twenty years Henry was rousted out of his bunk at seven in the morning. Nurses distributed sedatives and medications to those needing them. Then it was off to the dining room. Meals were served from trolleys. Normally breakfast consisted of hot cereal—porridge or Sunny Boy—toast, ham, and coffee, with a boiled egg once or twice a week.

After breakfast, chores had to be done. Most patients enjoyed helping, although no patient was ever forced to work. Those wanting to work were assigned simple tasks, such as helping with dishes, making beds (a job the patients did exceptionally well), folding laundry, washing and polishing floors, and a general cleaning once a week.

Some of the patients were then taken to their therapies. Others went out of doors in the airing courts, or for walks around the grounds when weather permitted. This was also the time for bathing. Bathrooms contained three tubs and a shower, but there was no loitering. Those who enjoyed soaking in a tub were out of luck. The nursing staff had to bathe twelve patients an hour. They came in as if on a conveyor belt in an assembly line, were scrubbed and rinsed, dried and pushed out, squeaky clean, to make room for the next one.

Dinner was served at eleven forty-five and usually consisted of vegetables, often turnips or parsnips, meatloaf or steamed fish, rhubarb or bread pudding and coffee.

After dinner the morning routine was repeated. Patients helped to clean up. Depending on the weather, they were taken to the airing court or for a walk. Some played cards in the day room. Others took a nap, but dorms were locked during the day, and patients were discouraged from sleeping in bed.

Nurses were not often available to socialize with the patients, as many would have liked. They were much too busy, doing menial chores, like washing windows, cleaning lockers, or writing reports in their unit record books. At the end of each shift, they were required to take a "sharp count." All utensils were carefully counted and secured to guard against self injury, suicide, or attacks on others.

At three, the afternoon shift came on. Medications were prepared and dispensed at four o'clock. Temperatures were taken.

Supper was light—a bowl of soup, a couple slices of bread, desert. Seldom was there anything green.

The dorms were opened at seven in the evening. Some of the patients went straight to bed. Others enjoyed a time of recreation. In the summer, many amassed at the softball diamond to watch a game. Very few of the patients played, but they liked to watch. Sometimes there would be a dance, but male and female patients were never allowed to mix.

Patients received refreshments at eight o'clock every evening. Bread and cocoa, hot chocolate or milk were served, after which, medication, to those needing it, was distributed. Then to bed.

Once or twice a night, patients, needing to go to the bathroom, were taken in groups. These night forays were known as "parades."

In the morning the routine started all over. Nothing differed from day to day, month to month, year to year. No variety. No adventure. No holiday. This was Henry's life.

The disease that maimed Henry's mind, later affected his spine, causing him difficulty in bending. In October of 1947, it began tearing at his heart, and he was transferred to ward 2 and 2B. The diagnosis was chronic myocarditus.

He came under the care of nurse Karl Leszynski, an immigrant from Poland who had served in World War II. He had been in Siberia and in most of Europe. He came to know Henry. Both spoke with European accents. Karl described Henry as a very quiet man, who, when he spoke, spoke slowly with some effort, but he was very friendly.

He often talked about the Temple and the house he built out of rocks, but Karl didn't pay much attention, believing that Henry's claims were nothing more than manifestations of delusions of grandeur. Karl knew a lot about that. He was in charge of a number of World War I veterans in the same ward with Henry, suffering from the same disease—syphilis. They had survived the war, but not the love making.

Karl was a kind and gentle man. In spite of his heavy work load, he tried to spend time talking to the patients. Henry was now too sick to push around a polishing block, and his attention span was short. Sometimes though, a rush of clarity opened his mind, and he could speak cogently and understand. He told Karl that he was Flemish and had lived in Belgium, near the Dutch border. Karl had been in Belgium and knew the country. This pleased Henry and he enjoyed asking Karl questions about his homeland. Then a nostalgic twinge of pain would spread over his face, and he'd fall silent, his eyes resting on his gnarled hands.

Nineteen-forty-eight was sort of a sunset year for Henry. He had come to terms with his condition and seemed relatively content. At least, he wasn't depressed.

He passed the time playing cribbage or dominos, but he seldom finished a game. For no apparent reason, he would get up from the table and shuffle away. He could not concentrate on anything for long.

Alberta Hospital Edmonton (Oliver) had gone through the hard times of the depression and the war years. The hospital was always skimping. If people were looking for jobs, the hospital didn't have sufficient funding to hire them. If funding was available, employees weren't. They were either off to the wars or making big money in the war industry. In 1948, there was neither depression nor war and certain amenities began to filter into the hospital.

Henry now occupied a ward with its own dining and recreation facilities. There was a crafts area and even a woodworking area. Henry took part in neither. Since leaving his Rock House and entering hospital, he never practiced his craft. He never worked with wood or glass or any other medium. He had crossed his Rubicon, abandoned his genius, and committed himself to oblivion. He would watch his fellow inmates doing crafts and woodwork, but he himself would not. He'd watch and then limp away. He suffered a paralyzed left side and had a problem bending. His disease was putting the final destructive touches to his spinal cord.

One day, nurse Joe Durocher noticed Henry in the woodshop. Someone had enticed him to operate the lathe. The skill and artistry, that had lain dormant for years, sprung to life. The magic returned. He quietly began to fashion spindles for a chair, using chisel and lathe. He mumbled incoherently as curls of wood peeled off the stock, transforming it into graceful contours. He measured nothing. The raw material simply evolved into a beautiful finished product, as if some internal genie operated Henry's appendages.

Joe Durocher could hardly believe his eyes. He watched spellbound as Henry produced his magic, as in earlier years. Joe never before paid much attention to Henry. He was just that quiet, uncommunicative patient who continually swung his hands back and forth and sequestered himself in a corner most of the day, mumbling incoherently.

He worked in the woodshop for awhile, and then no more. He gravitated to his corner and mumbled. Often the nurses had to physically remove him from the corner and take him to eat.

In spite of his discomforts, he seemed at ease with all his selves: the rebel boy, the gifted artisan, the unrequited lover, the unambitious dying man. The provincial public trustee provided him with a small allowance with which he bought chocolates, candy, and cigarettes. A quiet atmosphere permeated the ward. It was mostly occupied with old timers from the First World War. He also had a friend he would talk to in his lucid moments. His friend worked in the kitchen and would often bring him a cup of coffee.

Henry became weaker; his heart laboured harder. An oxygen tent became his last place of residence. Then one day, he had enough. On May 22, 1949, Henry Hoet made his escape. He slipped away quietly and unnoticed as was his wont. His tortured soul rose silently from his ravaged body, and it ached no more. The priest was called. He administered the last rites. The doctor pronounced him dead and signed his name, Martin M. Gish.

Two months earlier on March 3, 1949, the young lady who once became the centre of Henry's affections and illusions, died in a Calgary hospital of a perforated colon. Loila was forty-three years old. She had never married. She was buried in the Cardston Cemetery.

12. Cobblestone Manor

FOR nearly twenty years, the Rock house stood empty and boarded up. Time, the elements, and vandalism unremittingly assaulted its fortress-like walls. Some rot and decay invaded the interior. But, the house was well built and, though abandoned and uncared-for, it resisted the natural ruin that would have taken a lesser structure.

At last, in 1959, a buyer was found. The Masons sold the Rock House for $2,500 to Henry Schultz, a rancher from Pincher Creek. After nearly twenty years of silence, the sounds of voices and activity again reverberated within the rock walls. Repairs were made, and it became a home.

It then passed into the hands of RCMP Constable Lloyd Whittaker and his wife Jo-Anne in about 1972. They in turn sold it to William and Jacqueline Pitts in 1974.

In 1977, Edar Enterprises Ltd., owned by Ed and Arlene Flickinger, bought the estate. At the time, they owned and operated a successful restaurant in Turner Valley. Over the years their business had grown from a hamburger joint, featuring a huge hamburger called the trail boss, to a steak house, which became a favorite eating place in the area. They also did catering.

At one time, about a half-a-dozen Mormon families lived in Turner Valley, but, over the years, most of them had moved away. Ed and Arlene are Mormon. They felt more and more isolated as their Mormon friends moved elsewhere. They made good and lasting friends among the non-Mormon community, but they felt they needed the association and support of friends sharing their faith. Moreover, they had five children that they wanted to raise in a Mormon environment. Cardston, with the temple located at its centre, was, of course, the ideal place. So, Ed began to search for a place to establish a restaurant in Cardston. To his pleasant surprise, he learned that the Rock House was for sale. Ed knew the house. Shortly after receiving a diploma in hydrology, he took a job surveying the Chief Mountain Watershed for the Alberta government. While working in the Cardston area, he had frequent occasions to admire the Rock House and to imagine how it would be to own such a grand house, but he never believed it would ever be possible.

Now it was for sale, and Ed inquired about it. Allen Williams, the real estate salesman, responded negatively:

"Oh yes, that house has been up for sale for years."

"I'd still like to see it," insisted Ed. *What an ideal place for a restaurant,* he thought.

Ed was so thrilled with the prospect of owning the Rock House that he failed to notice its state of disrepair and the expense and labour it would require to restore it. Maybe he didn't want to notice it. Like Henry, who, years before, had gazed upon a drab log building amidst a site of ruin and rubble and saw a grand mansion, Ed envisioned a grand manor house that would, one day, be a fine and unique dining place—a place that would attract visitors from far and wide. While others viewed this massive rock formation as an impractical extravagance, Ed saw it as an expression of beauty that people would someday recognize as an object of great art.

Ed did not have much money, but he was determined to have that house if possible. He put down a two hundred dollar deposit and returned to his home in Turner Valley to spring the news on his wife, Arlene.

Arlene had been a teacher in the public school system for a while before raising kids and going into business with Ed. She is the more practical of the two, and, at a glance can discern the advantages and disadvantages of a project. She is also outspoken and skillful in her choice of words. And her words flowed like Lee's Creek, during spring run-off, when Ed took her to see the Rock House. She was neither impressed nor amused, when she inspected the structure and realized the years of backbreaking labour it would take to fully restore it.

Why does this man insist on doing everything the hard way? She thought as she wound her way through the maze of rooms, all requiring serious repair. *Will he never stop thinking of new things to do?*

Restoration presented a problem, but an even more daunting one emerged, like a sledge-hammer to the middle of the face. A number of people, living in Cardston, did not want any new development in the town, and that included the Flickinger's proposed restaurant. They circulated a petition, requesting that the town council deny the Flickingers proposal to establish a restaurant. The council responded by voting against the Flickinger's proposal six to one.

The dream seemed to die there. Ed and Arlene returned to their steak house in Turner Valley. Then, one day, a group of influential-looking men entered the steak house and seated themselves at one of the tables. They were from Cardston and looked familiar. One was Don Remington, the wealthy and influential rancher who possessed a love for fine horses and a fascination for restoring carriages. He was also interested in Ed's proposal to establish a restaurant in the Rock House. He and his entourage listened attentively to Ed as he described, with renewed enthusiasm, his plans for the Rock House.

Remington liked what he heard and suggested that Ed resubmit his request to town council. This he did, and the council responded by voting six to one in favor of the proposal—the exact reverse of the original vote.

Dreams overrode practicality and good sense, and Henry's dream house gained the chance for a future. It became Cobblestone Manor. As for the Flickingers, they bought a lifetime of hard work—of never-ending toil—reminiscent of Henry's work regimen. But it became a labour of love for both Ed and Arlene, and a place around which their family would grow and flourish and learn the value honest labour.

Shortly after the Flickingers bought the house, the council gave Ed and Arlene the invalid petition that their neighbours had signed to stop the use of the property for a restaurant. Ed and Arlene never looked at the document. One day while burning trash, they tossed the sealed envelope, containing the petition, into the fire, and that was the end of it. The community came to accept Cobblestone Manor, and to look upon this Provincial Historic Site with pride.

The house was in bad need of repair. It was much worse than either Ed or Arlene had first thought. Repairs alone would end up costing as much as the purchase price. The Flickingers worked seven months before the manor could be opened for business. During those months, they faced many frustrating barriers.

The entire roof needed replacing. Oddly, most of the house had two roofs, one on top of the other. Even so, it still leaked. Henry was a fine artist, but he was not a good planner. There was no consistency concerning the pitch of the gable or shed roofs. Each had a different pitch according to Henry's whim. The roofs over the verandahs were too shallow and did not stand up well under the harsh Alberta climate. Sixteen-inch squares of tin, soldered together, covered one layer of roof. Henry laid the two-by-four rafters at random distances, some up to nearly a metre apart. Working on the roof was tantamount to placing your life in extreme danger. You could fall through at any time, without warning. All the rafters needed replacing.

Only now did Ed realize what he had gotten himself into. Fixing the roof didn't just mean shingling, it meant replacing the entire roof, including rafters. It also meant increasing the pitch of the roofs on all the verandahs to better shed snow. Moreover, money was limited.

Many negatives were beginning to pile up. Just when things looked their worst, up drove Leonard, one of the best roofers in southern Alberta.

Leonard was from Turner Valley and a friend of the Flickingers. Flashing his toothless grin, Leonard climbed out of his pick-up truck and limped painfully on bowed legs toward Ed, his hand extended. Though he was unexpected, he was more than welcome, and he couldn't have come at a better time. Ed needed a roof and Leonard needed work and a place to park his camping trailer—presently his permanent home. He knew the Flickingers would accommodate him.

After many years of marriage and raising two sons, Leonard's wife left him. Adding to the pain of his loss, he suffered terribly from arthritis. The disease horribly deformed his joints. Horse lineament seemed to be the only thing that relieved his discomfort, and he rubbed the odoriferous liquid into his knees in great quantities. He also smoked like a prairie brush fire. The lineament and tobacco together gave Leonard a distinctive odor he wore like a brand.

Leonard earned his keep. He was a hard worker, in spite of his constant pain, and a good friend. He would rest the ladder in the middle of the roof and work toward one end. At that point, the ladder would be at a precarious slant and balancing on one leg in complete defiance of gravity. Then he would do the same toward the other end.

When work on the roof was finished, Leonard got other roofing jobs in Cardston. He kept busy and constantly on the move. He continued to live in his camping trailer on Flickingers property. Never one to worry about his health, Leonard overworked himself, caught a chill, and came down with a bad case of pneumonia. Arlene did everything possible to get him to see a doctor, but he resisted. Finally, in desperation, she called Dr. Bob Russell, a local doctor, and explained Leonard's condition. The doctor hurried right over, examined Leonard, and prescribed medication for him, but he didn't stop there. Dr. Russell saw Leonard as a man in pain and in need of help. Through his influence, he obtained a small government pension for Leonard, even though he had not yet reached retirement age. He also managed to get him a room at the Senior Citizen's Lodge, where, for a time, he lived happily and contented. The only drawback was that he was not allowed to smoke inside the lodge. He had to go outside for that. He eventually left the lodge and moved back to Turner Valley with his sons.

Help in renovating Cobblestone Manor also came from another source, an old friend by the name of John P. Hanson. John owned a contracting company in High River and had helped the Flickingers build various buildings in Turner Valley. Now, he was well into his mid-seventies and the one and only employee in his company. He was still very active and had lived a long and colourful life. He grew up at Waterton and had worked on the Prince of Wales Hotel, and, while he knew of Henry, he didn't know him personally.

John's father had owned a sawmill in Waterton and had known Kootenai Brown. Kootenai's wife, Isabella (Chee-pay-tha-quaka-soon), a Cree princess, gave John's father a Cree name.

When John learned that the Flickingers had bought the Rock House in Cardston and planned to establish another restaurant there, it brought back old memories, including tales of Henry Hoet. He loved the old Rock House, and when the Flickingers needed a contractor to comply with the demands of the mortgage company, John was right there to offer his services. He took up temporary residence in Cobblestone Manor and helped Ed with the renovations.

In the process of reroofing Cobblestone Manor, Ed and John discovered that the ceiling insulation consisted of sawdust. Over the years the sawdust often became wet, causing mildew and widespread rotting of the ceiling underlay to which the honey combed panels were attached in the Golden Oak Room. John, Ed and Arlene had to remove about a third of the ceiling panels, piece by piece. They numbered each panel and, after replacing the rotten rafters and underlay, they reassembled the panels as if it were a jig saw puzzle. The three of them worked an entire month on that project.

Time and the elements had also attacked some of the rectangular wall panels in the golden oak room. This presented a problem. Where could one obtain golden oak veneer? Was there anything Ed could substitute for it?

While taking care of business in Lethbridge, Ed stopped in at Advanced Lumber Company, a store he knew Henry dealt with when he was building his house, and asked the manager if they had any sheets of golden oak. The manager said that they had never carried anything like that, but one of the older employees overheard the conversation and mentioned seeing some stashed away in the back of the building behind other materials. They had been there for years.

Sure enough, they were there—fifteen sheets in all. They appeared to match perfectly those used in

Cobblestone Manor. They were of an odd size. Instead of the standard four-by-eight sheets, these were four-by-seven, suggesting that they probably came from somewhere other than Canada or the United States. It seems probable that they were the same sheets of oak Henry himself had ordered years before, but never had a chance to claim before his sickness overtook him. Ed couldn't believe his luck. He loaded the unexpected booty in his pick-up truck and headed home. When John saw the golden oak panels, he all but jumped for joy. After replacing all the damaged golden oak, only a half-a-sheet remained.

John became totally absorbed with his work on Cobblestone Manor and lovingly restored so much of Henry's work. In the process, he and the Flickingers became very close friends. After the restaurant opened for business, John returned and stayed at Cobblestone Manor many times before his death.

The cost of renovations had taken a heavy toll on the Flickinger's finances, but, now, the major repairs were behind them. They seemed to have entered calmer waters. A few more minor repairs and the restaurant would be ready for the grand opening.

Some of the lamps' stained glass was broken or missing, but the Flickingers found a number of pieces in the attic. There were enough to use all original glass in the restoration, even though some of the pieces had cracks.

None of the original lamps remained in the golden oak room, and no one remembers if they resembled those installed in the dark oak room. There remained, however, outlets in the ceiling. Conduit, as would be required in commercial buildings, surrounded the wiring leading to the outlets. All the wiring in the room had been damaged and needed replacing. Ed installed lighting fixtures of a more modest kind in the golden oak room than were found in the dark oak room. To make replicas of Henry's stained glass lamps would have been economically prohibitive, even if the Flickingers could have found someone capable of doing the job. That was not likely. It is also doubtful that the Flickingers could even locate stained glass that would match the glass used by Henry.

The Flickingers, with the help of friends and family, had restored the house, as close to its original condition as possible, and they finished what Henry had left unfinished in his style.

They were ready to open for business when in strolled a building inspector with an unabridged building code manual etched into his frontal lobe. He didn't say much. His utterances consisted mainly of ahems and grunts. Then, pointing at the ceiling, he announced imperiously, "That's gotta go." The certainty in his voice left no hope for compromise or negotiation. He delivered the order as if it were a ukase from which there could be no appeal.

Ed and Arlene stood dumb-struck. They had done everything possible to maintain and enhance the integrity of the house in a manner that would be consistent with Henry Hoet's work. The intricate honey-combed panels, Henry had slaved over, were an essential part of the whole. To tear them out would not only be an esthetic crime; it would be an obscenity, like cropping the sky out of a Van Gough.

Ed's stubborn streak kicked in. There was no way he was going to commit the atrocity of ripping out the ceiling and replacing it with some bland synthetic product that would meet the crass taste of a Teflon bureaucrat. He took his case and the plans of Cobblestone Manor straight to the buildings code division in Edmonton and argued against having to remove the panels. But he was getting nowhere. He became persistent and insistent on his point. At this impasse an older civil servant overheard the altercation and intervened.

"I'll take care of this," he said to the younger man.

He listened as, again, Ed explained the importance of maintaining the integrity of the house. The elderly gentleman, himself a connoisseur of fine old buildings, understood and sympathized with Ed's plight. More than that, he agreed with him.

"Mr. Flickinger," he said, "you follow me and let me do all the talking."

Taking Ed in tow, he led him into each department. He laid out the plans in front of the persons in charge, said a few words, and got them approved. Ed said not a word. In each department he stood silently beside the old gentleman like a department store mannequin. Soon, the ordeal was over and Ed returned to Cardston with all of his plans stamped approved.

To satisfy board of health standards, Ed added a new kitchen and changed the fireplaces to meet fire regulations. Not wanting to disturb the originality of the building, Ed built an addition to the house that included a large foyer and rest rooms.

Unfortunately, Henry Hoet did not make the furniture that is now in Cobblestone Manor. The furniture that Henry built is distributed throughout the Cardston area. The Masons own the largest collection of Henry's furniture. It is presently in use at their meeting hall in Cardston. However, in keeping with the style and spirit of Henry's aesthetic tastes, the Flickingers purchased fine antiques from England and Holland to furnish Cobblestone Manor's three dining rooms.

It took two months for the furniture to arrive. During that time, the Flickingers waited anxiously, reminiscent to when Henry waited anxiously for his stained glass and other exotic building materials to arrive from Europe. When the furniture did arrive, the Flickingers were more than pleased. Every piece complimented Henry's style. Nothing looked out of place. Included in their assortment of antique furniture was a nine-foot solid oak table.

The day of the Grand Opening finally came, and, for once, everything came together without a hitch. And, in keeping with the unusual events that seemed to always be connected with Cobblestone Manor, the Grand Opening featured another such event. Don Remington, the man instrumental in paving the way for the establishment of Cobblestone Manor as a restaurant, arrived at the Grand Opening with an entourage of guests, six couples including Don and his wife.

They arrived in a gorgeous Park Drag Carriage, drawn by four matched black horses. The gentlemen and their wives alit from the carriage in nineteenth century Victorian style. The women wore elegant long dresses and large colourful hats, while the men donned tuxedos. With his taste for grandeur, Henry would have appreciated this.

In 1995, Ed converted the living room of the original log house (the Henry Hoet room) into a gift shop. It occupies the centre of the house with access from the Golden Oak Room.

Today Cobblestone Manor is a honeycombed hive of constant activity. When Ed is not cooking, he is either building or repairing the manor. "All of our children have worked in the Cobblestone Manor," said Arlene, "sometimes reluctantly. But, Ed and I always felt good about it, because we had chores for them to do."

Sons and daughters include: Terrilyn, an interior designer who decorated the interior of Cobblestone Manor and who sometimes cooks. Arlene says, "As good as her dad." Gerald (Jerry) and his wife Kim are both health care workers and have three children. Debra lives in Utah with her husband and three children. Michael also lives in Utah with his wife and four children. Brad and his wife Monique own and run a monthly newspaper, the *Legend*, that serves all of southern Alberta. They continue to work at Cobblestone Manor. They have one daughter.

Each of the children held their wedding receptions at Cobblestone Manor.

Grandchildren visit frequently and there are thirteen in all. Added to this sizable family, friends, young and old, often visit the Cobblestone Manor. Some even take up residence for varying lengths of time.

Under the auspices of Ed and Arlene, Cobblestone Manor exudes a feeling of friendliness and warmth. It permeates the paneled rooms. One is made to feel comfortable here, surrounded with a homey, sincere attitude that you are welcome. Cobblestone Manor is today governed by a loving, extended family that puts on no airs, and, when you are among them, you are treated as one of them, not as a visitor.

In the evening the lights shining through Henry's stained glass lamps cast a mellow glow. The intricate panels draw in and mesmerize the viewer. One feels the presence of the quiet, gentle builder who created this multi-dimensional work of art. It is not just something that is seen; it is felt. It projects and personifies the immortality of the human spirit and its creative capacity long after the physical aspects are dust.

Arlene Flickinger admits that she believes Henry's presence still occupies the house.

"I think he's happy," she says. "It's a better purpose to the house, where so much of the public can see his work. They [Alberta Culture] do want the house preserved, and it should be."

The Alberta government designated the house a historic site in 1983.

Afterword

HENRY Hoet never formed any close friendships while living in Cardston. He preferred isolation. This was his choice. Certainly there were a number of people in Cardston who would have been happy to strike up a lasting friendship with him. Many people in the community held an affection for this solitary man. But he remained locked in his own world into which he allowed no one to enter.

It appears that Henry became enamored with Loila Williams, but those feelings also remained locked in the prison of his mind, except for occasional leaks to his friend Charley. It is most probable that Loila never realized the effect she produced on Henry. Her short courtship with her boyfriend from Chicago must have left her with sufficient pain of her own.

Loila was not one to dwell on her own problems. She thrust her energies into living a very active and productive life. She continued to teach in the area, but her teaching career was sporadic. She also continued to upgrade her education.

In 1934 the Mormon Church called upon her to serve as a missionary in the Pacific northwest. She jumped at the opportunity and served in Vancouver, British Columbia and Portland, Oregon. She was a missionary for two years.

Her primary interest continued to be art and, in September of 1936, she enrolled in art classes at Brigham Young University in Utah, where her art was prominently displayed in the Arts Building.

Her delicate health demanded that she limit her active life. Her family pleaded with her to slow down. Her brother Shem wrote her the following letter that indicated the state of her declining health. At this time she probably suffered from chronic colitis.

> Now as for yourself, how about worrying about your little self. If you could study endocarditus instead of hop scotch, you'd become convinced of certain things but since you haven't & arn't, let me draw you a few conclusions. Not to worry you but to impress certain facts.......
>
> Now I am advising you not to overdo & keep up your bodily resistance by eating plenty of good food & a couple of malted milks in between then remember it isn't nearly so important what you eat as your mental attitude. Here is a sentence directly from my physiology. "Cannon found that all movements of the stomach ceased as soon as the animal showed signs of anxiety, rage or distress." Now just you keep that $5.00 [Shem had sent her the $5.00] to induce stomach movements when you start to get worried & full of stress. Take it out, stroke it a few times & put it back in your sock till the next meal or something.

She returned home and took a job teaching in Cardston School. In 1949 she underwent an operation at Holy Cross Hospital in Calgary and never recovered. She died on March 3, 1949. She was Forty-three years old. She is buried in the Cardston Cemetery next to her mother Attena who died two years before her. A simple bronze plaque marks her place.

For Henry Hoet there is no epitaph; there is no marker. There is only an aisle of grass, running approximately fifty metres, parallel to the infants' graves. The isle ends at a chain link fence beyond which is a road and an apartment complex. There aren't many trees in this section of the cemetery. A solemn quiet reaches over the area like an invisible fog, and matted golden autumn leaves, the hue of his golden oak room, lay strewn and moldering on the ground, blown there by the wind from the more heavily wooded areas of the cemetery. It is quiet but for the hum of traffic on the highway, running adjacent the St. Joachim's Cemetery in Edmonton, Alberta. It is quiet but for the occasional burst of rock music, emitted from the high decibel speakers from the trunk of a passing car.

Henry Hoet lies in a common grave designated as Grave 495, Sec.13. He is buried with two others whose lives, as his, ended in poverty and anonymity. Henry Hoet now lies in an unmarked grave, having been given a twenty dollar funeral in 1949, compliments of the Province of Alberta. Andrews-McLaughlin, located on Jasper Avenue and 112 Street, served as funeral director and took care of arrangements.

Henry Hoet was insolvent. Therefore, the Administrator of Estates for the Mentally Incompetent closed his file at the time of his death.

Even though long and extensive research has gone into the search for Henry's family, not one member has been found. Months of research has not turned up anything about his life in Belgium. His life passed over the horizon like a phantom's. And perhaps that's the way he preferred it. But he did leave behind a monument to celebrate the human will to love, dream and create. Out of his progressively deteriorating mind, he contemplated beauty and translated it into a tangible form. He is dust, but the rock and wood and glass he molded with his toil and genius will stand firmly into the ages as evidence of human creativity and will.

And, according to Arlene Flickinger, his quiet and humble spirit still occupies Cobblestone Manor.

Bibliography

Abercrombie, Sheila. *Alberta Hospital Edmonton 1923 to 1983: An Outline History to Commemorate the 60th Anniversary.* Edmonton: Alberta Hospital Edmonton, 1983. This work proved an invaluable source, not only for the historical and descriptive account of the hospital, but also for identifying many of the people who worked there during Henry's hospitalization. I interviewed many of these people, some of whom knew and cared for Henry Hoet.

Alberta Justice Department, File: 4373L.

Alberta Provincial Police. Letters. Henry Hoet File, Alberta Justice Department.

"Cardston's House of Dreams." *Waterton Glacier Views.* Aug. 3, 1994.

Chaplin, James P. *Dictionary of Psychology.* New York: Dell Publishing Co., Inc., 1968.

Chief Mountain Country: A History of Cardston and District. Vol. I. Cardston, Alberta: Cardston and District Historical Society, 1978.

Chief Mountain Country: A History of Cardston and District. Vol. II. Cardston, Alberta: Cardston and District Historical Society, 1987

Church of Jesus Christ of Latter-Day Saints in Canada. *A History of the Mormon Church in Canada.* Lethbridge, Alberta: Lethbridge Herald Co., 1968.

Djuff, Ray. *The Prince of Wales Hotel.* ed. by Chris Morrison. Waterton Park, Alberta: Waterton Natural History Association, 1991. This book provided much of the material dealing with the Prince of Wales Hotel. It is the most complete work on the hotel that I have been able to find.

Downs, Art (ed.) Waterton National Park. Surrey, B.C.: Frontier Books, 1980.

Encyclopædia Britannica. 15th Edition. Chicago: Encyclopædia Britannica, Inc., 1980.

Fooks, Georgia Green. "Cobblestone Manor becomes an Historic Site." Lethbridge, Fall 1983.

Gibb, R. Michael of Gowling and Gibb Architects, in Calgary. "Project architect for the restoration of the Alberta Temple," Historical Department, The Church of Jesus Christ of Latter-day Saints. The James Moyle Oral History Program. R. Michael Gibb Interviewed by Brian D. Reeves, Calgary,

Alberta, Canada and Salt Lake City, Utah, July 19 and October 3, 1991.

Hudson, James A. *Charles Ora Card: Pioneer and Colonizer.* Cardston, Alberta: published by author, 1963.

Massey, R.M. "The Cobblestone Manor." Prepared for Alberta Culture, Historical Resources, Historic Sites Service., August 1981.

Nielson, Olive Wood. *A Treasury of Edward J. Wood.* Salt Lake City, Utah: Publishers Press, 1983.

Oland, Doug. *Memoirs.* Author and journalist Ray Djuff provided me with a copy of Oland's *Memoirs.* I drew extensively on these *Memoirs* for the information appearing in chapter 6.

Packer, Boyd K. The *Holy Temple.* Salt Lake City: Bookcraft, 1980.

Pringle, Heather. *A Guide to Waterton Lakes National Park.* Vancouver: Douglas & McIntyre, 1986.

Province of Alberta Registration of Death of Henry Hoet.

Restak, Richard M., M.D. *The Brain.* New York: Bantam Books, 1984.

Sprague, D.N. *Post-Confederation Canada: The Structure of Canadian History Since 1867.* Scarborough, Ontario: Prentice-Hall Canada Inc.,1990.

Tagg, Melvin S. *The Life of Edward James Wood Church Patriot.* Master of Science Thesis presented to the College of Religious Instruction, Brigham Young University, 1959.

Wilcox, Archie G. "The founding of the Mormon Community in Alberta." Master's thesis, University of Alberta, 1950.

Williams, Loila. Unpublished Journal, letters, pictures and art work. This material was generously supplied by Loila's niece, Laura L. Barrus. Most of the information in this book about Loila came from her Journal. The story of the life of this remarkable woman begs to be told and would provide excellent subject matter for a book.

Wood, V.A. *The Alberta Temple: Centre and Symbol of Faith.* Calgary, Alberta: Detselig Enterprises Ltd., 1989.Wood's book has been an invaluable source of information and pictures concerning the Alberta Temple. Most of the information about the Temple and its construction I used came from Wood's book. It is the most comprehensive book on the Alberta Temple. It is written with warmth and knowledge from first hand experience.

Index

To Order

Grand Delusions: Henry Hoet and Cobblestone Manor

by

James Musson

Please send $14.95 plus $4.00 postage and handling to:

Brightest Pebble Publishing Co. Inc.
7604 - 149 Avenue
Edmonton, Alberta, Canada
T5C 2V7

Special prices apply for quantity purchases of 10 or more copies.

For special prices please call James Musson at (403) 457-7496